PRAISE FOR S' WORKFORCE PLANNING

'As the pace of business change intensifies, effective strategic workforce planning can be the difference between business success and business failure. Ross Sparkman is one of the leading authorities in the world on strategic workforce planning and this book is full of practical and stimulating advice. As such, I expect *Strategic Workforce Planning* to become an indispensable compendium for HR and business leaders alike to help steer their ability to thrive in the digital economy.'
David Green, Global People Analytics Leader, IBM

'Ross Sparkman has distilled the complex field of strategic workforce planning into its essential steps, using practical frameworks and exercises that accelerate the readers' understanding. This is a must-read for both new and experienced strategic workforce planning practitioners.' **Peter Louch, CEO, Vemo**

'This book is *the* definitive guide to strategic workforce planning. Brilliantly written by one of the most prominent global thought leaders in workforce planning, this is a must-read for both HR and business professionals, as well as anyone interested in finding out more about the practical application and science behind workforce planning and analytics.' **Stavros Demetriou, Director, People Analytics, major global consulting firm**

Strategic Workforce Planning

Developing optimized talent strategies
for future growth

Ross Sparkman

KoganPage

First published in Great Britain and the United States in 2018 by Kogan Page Limited

2nd Floor, 45 Gee Street	c/o Martin P Hill Consulting	4737/23 Ansari Road
London	122 W 27th St, 10th Floor	Daryaganj
EC1V 3RS	New York, NY 10001	New Delhi 110002
United Kingdom	USA	India

www.koganpage.com

ISBN   978 0 7494 8201 5
E-ISBN   978 0 7494 8202 2

British Library Cataloguing-in-Publication Data

A CIP record for this book is available from the British Library.

Library of Congress Cataloging-in-Publication Control Number

2017057696

Typeset by Integra Software Services, Pondicherry
Print production managed by Jellyfish
Printed and bound by CPI Group (UK) Ltd, Croydon, CR0 4YY

CONTENTS

Introduction

What this book is about

Strategic workforce planning (SWP; sometimes called workforce planning or talent planning) is not a new concept. In fact, at a fundamental level, the notion of planning future workforce requirements has been around for decades. What has changed, however, is the degree of detail and sophistication that some organizations now require when going through the activity of this planning. This book will take a closer look at some of the reasons why, in recent years, some organizations have levitated towards more detail and sophistication regarding their SWP, but whatever the case, these factors have led some organizations to emphasize developing a more rigorous approach to planning for their workforce requirements.

The intention of this book is to provide business and human resource (HR) leaders, along with SWP practitioners, with a menu of options to consider regarding how to plan out future workforce requirements. This book will provide different frameworks to use in the SWP process, it will provide discussions into the various areas of the organization that can potentially benefit from SWP, and it will give guidance on how to build a high-powering SWP function. In addition to these topics, the book will also discuss tactics on how to create and scale adoption of the SWP function across the organization and will provide commentary on trends in how the future of work can impact the SWP function's role in the company.

Who this book is for

At the most fundamental level, this is a business book. Consider it a tool for any business or HR leader who wants to put more strategic thought into how to create a more effective and productive workforce that supports the business's strategic objectives. This book also can be a supplemental tool for employees who are already operating as practitioners in the SWP space. For these individuals, the book can be thought of as an additional asset to include in their toolbox. It is aimed to help them to think through issues with a fresh 'set of eyes'. Finally, this book can function as a research tool for individuals or employees who might be looking for a career change where the idea of working in the strategic HR or the SWP space is something that they have considered and would like to learn about in more detail.

How to use this book

This book can be used as a comprehensive approach to learning about SWP where the reader will probably gain the most value by reading the book from cover to cover. The reader might also only be interested in certain portions of the book, such as understanding how to project workforce supply and demand, in which case there might be more value in reading only the relevant chapters. That said, the chapters in this book have been laid out in a fashion that allows the reader to jump in at any point to gain those relevant learnings. All of the chapters also contain a summary section at the end of the chapter that outlines the key learning objectives. Reading the summaries might be useful for readers who need to learn about the foundational aspects of SWP in a hurry, but do not have the time to read the book in its entirety.

Terminology used in the book

Throughout this book, there are several terms that will be used quite consistently. In some instances, the terms will be utilized interchangeably while, at other times, they will reflect particular nuances relating to the topic. To help alleviate any confusion on the part of the reader, the definitions of these terms are provided below:

Strategic workforce planning/SWP (broad definition): An activity or process relating to the workforce that an organization, team or function takes part in to develop, optimize or enhance that entity's ability to contribute to positive business outcomes.

Organization: Any organized group of people, employees or business leaders working towards a common goal. As it relates to this book, an organization tends to be the equivalent of a business, company or not-for-profit entity.

Function: An organized group of employees or individuals that support an organization or business in achieving its broader objectives – eg its corporate strategy.

Team: Can sometimes also refer to a function, but in the context of this book usually refers to a smaller set of employees within a function.

SWP practitioner: Refers to an individual or employee whose job is either partly or solely in support of SWP.

SWP team: This term is used interchangeably with 'SWP function' in this book, but can also refer to a sole SWP practitioner.

SWP function: In the context of this book, this term can be used interchangeably with 'SWP team', but tends to be slightly larger, more matrixed or more mature in nature compared to the definition of a SWP team provided above.

Strategic workforce planning

01

CHAPTER OBJECTIVES

1 Define SWP and its practical application for companies and organizations.
2 Define the purpose and benefits of SWP.
3 Outline the challenges of SWP.
4 Outline structuring of an SWP function.
5 Outline key jobs, roles and skills involved in SWP.

What is strategic workforce planning?

Fundamentally, the easiest way to define SWP is to drop the first two words in the term 'strategic workforce planning' and explore the meaning of the last word 'planning'. Doing so in the context of the organization's people will provide a much more intuitive explanation as to what SWP is. SWP at the most fundamental level is a framework for analysing both the current and desired future states of the workforce. Assessing these different workforce states across different points in time will provide insight into what, if any, gaps exist between where the company is with its people today, and where it should be with those same people in the future. If done properly and with the right support and direction, this type of analysis will shed light on specific areas in the workforce that require attention to achieve that desired state. Identifying improvements is the first step in a guideline towards specific action steps that need to be taken towards the desired future state. For example, suppose the fictional company Widgets-Are-Us decides to embark on an SWP assessment. The company starts by looking at its current workforce structure in key verticals across the business. It does this by analysing some basic workforce metrics like average tenure and age. This simple analysis reveals that, within the engineering function, 70 per cent of the workforce are over the age of 50, with 60 per cent of that workforce possessing over 20 years' experience.

Let us assume that the next step in this assessment involves looking into how future aspects of the broader organizational strategy could impact on the company's people strategy. This part of the analysis revealed that the Research and Development (R&D) team had developed some breakthrough products that will leverage 3D print technology. This new technology is a massive opportunity for Widgets-Are-Us and will position the company for success in a whole new niche market in the widgets industry. The catch, however, is that this new 3D print technology will require a new set of skills in the engineering function.

From an SWP standpoint, we now have two clear themes that have emerged from the analysis. The first key finding is that the company's engineering function is clearly at risk of losing a large portion of its knowledge base due to impending retirements. The second is that, not only will there be a gap in current skills within this function, but also there will be a gap in future skills required for the company's new strategic direction.

The next step in this fictional example would be to develop a detailed plan to mitigate against the impending risk of a potential knowledge and skills gap. It is here that the strategic part of SWP comes into play. SWP practitioners, human resource business partners (HRBPs) and business leaders will need to collaborate on developing a plan of key actions, timelines and deliverables required to ensure that systems, processes and owners are in place to mitigate these two risks. A simple Strategic Workforce Plan in this example might seek to answer such questions as the following:

Knowledge drain

- What are the key skills that will be lost due to impending retirements?
- How do we ensure we have captured the knowledge that these employees possess once they leave?
- Do we have a system in place to capture these skills?
- If not, how would a system look?
    - Is it a technology?
    - Is it training material developed for new employees by the retirees?
- Is there an opportunity to bring these retirees on as part-time consultants?

3D print technology

- How do we assess the skills needed for effective 3D print technology?
- Can we build on skills that are already in place?
- Do these skills exist in the external labour market?
- Can we develop a training programme to develop these skills?
- Would it be more cost-effective to buy or build these required skills?
- Are there other companies that either have or are developing these skills?
- How much are these skills worth in the external labour market?
- What is the impact to the business if we are unable to develop or acquire these skills?
- What is the timeline for when these skills will be required?

The preceding bullet points are examples of the strategic questions that a good Strategic Workforce Plan should address, but that is just the beginning. A good Strategic Workforce Plan will not only address the strategic questions but also outline the plan's execution in detail. In essence, it will be a comprehensive project plan that has clear owners, with defined timelines, action items, deliverables and outcomes for success. It should also provide metrics success and risk metrics, as well as outlining a communication and change-management plan. Operational questions in a Strategic Workforce Plan that require significant thought include:

- Who are the stakeholders that need to be involved in the plan's action steps?
- Who will sponsor the plan?
- Is there an executive sponsor in place?
- Will a steering committee or project team be established?
- Will there be an ongoing meeting rhythm established?
- What is the timeline for the plan?
- What are the specific actions that need to take place?
- What are the plan's success metrics?
- Will the plan require change management?
- Will the plan be across all locations or more targeted?
- How much time and effort will be required to execute the plan?
- How will the roles and responsibilities for the plan be decided?
- What are the costs associated with the plan/project?
- How will these costs be measured and tracked?

So, to answer the original question: SWP is the process of thinking through the challenges and opportunities that an organization's people could/will face as market conditions change and business cycles mature (see Figure 1.1). It seeks to define how the organization's workforce structure should evolve as these market conditions change and the business develops. Simply put, SWP is the function within a company tasked with identifying people-related opportunities and challenges associated with changes to the business, then developing a plan to capitalize on the opportunities and mitigate the risks linked to those changes.

What SWP is not

SWP is not a silver bullet that will solve all the challenges that an organization faces. Rather, it is a map that can help to guide the business

Figure 1.1 Fundamentals of SWP

towards some desired state. To that end, executive sponsorship is very important. There needs to be a sense of organizational commitment and a willingness to see the plan executed from start to finish. It is also not a simple 'one-size-fits-all' methodology or framework. In fact, an important part of the SWP process involves understanding – in the context of the organizational culture – how to customize and develop a plan that will meet the cultural nuances and operating processes of that organization. The organization should approach the plan with a level of creativity and openness to interpretation. Good SWP is not something that will happen overnight; hence the need for commitment. Embedding SWP into a cross-functional, enterprise-wide operating process takes time. Moreover, realizing and being able to measure the impact and return on investment (ROI) of SWP will require even more time.

For an organization that has laid out a five-year Strategic Workforce Plan, it is not unreasonable to see the net benefits to the company for up to two to five years after the initial execution of the plan. It is necessary to think of SWP as being a cultural shift towards becoming an organization that is proactive and future facing. It is also something that will probably not be well understood by the masses. Like implementing any new initiative, process or programme in an organization, it is likely to face significant resistance due to paradigm shifts in thinking (Lewin, 2008). Anticipating this resistance by incorporating a well thought-out change management and communications strategy as part of the broader Strategic Workforce Plan will greatly increase the likelihood of a successful implementation.

While workforce analytics is an important aspect of SWP (there will be an entire chapter (Chapter 10) in this book dedicated to workforce analytics), there is much more to it than just the analytics. As it relates to SWP, it is often useful to think of workforce analytics as the biggest tool in the SWP toolkit. It is the data and analysis portion of the SWP process that will help the organization to understand key gaps in current versus future workforce structure. Identifying and understanding these gaps cannot be accomplished without a level of data and analysis. When it comes to analytics in SWP, it is worth noting how broad the spectrum between sophisticated and basic the analyses can be. It can be something as simple as plotting tenure across a histogram on one end of the spectrum to developing sophisticated machine learning algorithms designed to predict employee-level attrition on the other.

Finally, SWP will not be easy. The more time, effort and commitment invested in the plan in the long term, the more effective the planning will be at helping the organization align its people with its strategy. It is not easy to develop and execute a Strategic Workforce Plan in a couple of days or even weeks. There are many dimensions and 'moving parts' that require thought. The development and nurturing of cross-functional relationships and partnerships is imperative. Data will have to be structured and analysed. Also, developing project plans and allocating resources can make or break the success of a project. These things all take time and patience, which is why it is so important to have the commitment and vision in place before diving head on into the process of developing an SWP function and ultimately a Strategic Workforce Plan.

The purpose and benefits of SWP

What is the purpose of SWP? There will be a discussion on this in future chapters. But for now, at a high level, the purpose of SWP is to improve the performance of the company or organization (see Figure 1.2). Improving the organization's performance through its people can be achieved by better alignment of skills, programmes, teams and day-to-day work with the strategy, objectives and goals of that company or organization (Noe *et al*, 2003).

Figure 1.2   Improve company performance by aligning the workforce with the corporate strategy

To help illustrate this point, let us go back to our fictional company, Widgets-Are-Us, and explore an example of what this might look like for a typical company. We know that Widgets-Are-Us is a company that manufactures widgets. We also know that, to remain competitive and innovative in its industry, the company must continue to bring newer and better products to market faster than its competitors. Doing this requires the company to invest heavily in R&D and the newest technologies. From our earlier example, we learned that the company has decided to invest heavily in 3D print technology, so much so that the organization has shifted a large part of its strategy to developing more customized products created through 3D print technology. Because the company's longer-term strategy will change, it is important to note that the change will also have an impact on the company's longer-term workforce strategy. Let us examine how this new strategy might affect certain processes in the HR function. For starters, the recruiting team will need to understand the profile of candidates they will be required to source from a background and experience perspective, while HR business partners will need to understand the necessary skill sets for optimal performance of the new strategy. They will also need to understand how this new product approach will affect the traditional manufacturing processes in place. There also will be additional questions that arise, for example:

- Will this new strategic direction have an impact on the size and headcount requirements for the organization's traditional manufacturing workforce?
- Will there be a reduction in the size of this workforce or will the employees in these more traditional roles be cross-trained to meet the operational requirements of 3D print technology?
- How about location, will the new product strategy call for a more geographically dispersed workforce?

  - If so, will this require current employees to transfer?
  - Could this have an impact on attrition?
  - Would attrition be a good or a bad thing?

- How will the cost structure of this new workforce compare to the past workforce structure?
- Will these more specialized skills require higher levels of compensation?
- Will a 3D print technology strategy require more or fewer employees than the current manufacturing process?
- What is the typical profile of an employee with 3D print technology experience?

  - Do they prefer to be contractors or freelancers?
  - Consequently, does the company need to develop a contingent workforce strategy?

From these questions, it becomes apparent that a simple change in strategy has the potential to have a profound impact on the structure of the company's workforce. At a minimum, it raises some philosophical workforce-related questions that require answers. In addition to these fundamental questions, it sheds light on the fact that a change of strategy does, in fact, impact the workforce. How the organization deals with the new workforce requirements will be a major deciding factor as to whether the new strategic direction is successful.

The point of this example is to illustrate that making organizational strategy decisions in a vacuum, without considering the impact of these decisions on the workforce, can lead to ignoring one of the biggest factors that could make or break the success of that new strategy. It is here that we can start to see the true purpose of SWP, which is to ensure that the right questions are being asked and answered with regards to how the organization's workforce will contribute to the success of its current and future strategies, subsequently resulting in the development of a robust plan to address these questions.

The benefits of SWP across the organization

SWP benefits the organization because it provides managers, leaders and HR professionals with insights regarding the current and future state of the workforce. Workforce insights of this nature provide these managers, leaders and HR professionals with the information they need to make optimal workforce-related decisions. Having the knowledge and ability to make the best decisions for the organization's workforce, in turn, will lead to cost-effectiveness, efficiency gains and performance improvement for the organization (Wood, Bandura and Bailey, 1990). SWP is also a mechanism for bridging the gap between the organization's corporate strategy and its workforce strategy. Aligning corporate and workforce strategies is crucial for maximizing future company performance. This is because so much of the organization's corporate strategy is dependent on having a workforce in place that has the talent necessary to execute on the strategy's objectives. Developing a workforce with this talent begins with alignment of the workforce and corporate strategies, which is exactly what SWP helps the organization to do.

What parts of an organization stand to benefit most from SWP? A better question might be to ask: what parts of the organization will not benefit from SWP? The purpose of SWP is to align the current and future workforce with the organization's strategy. The organizational strategy is dependent upon the separate components or functions of the business, which are in turn dependent on the people working in these functions. It is easy to see why every aspect of the business stands to benefit from SWP.

A good Strategic Workforce Plan should look across the entire organization to see how, within these functions, employees – both at an individual and a group level – contribute to improving the organization's performance (see Figure 1.3). Looking across the organization as described above provides the SWP practitioner with insight into

Figure 1.3   A good SWP process operates across different levels
of the organization

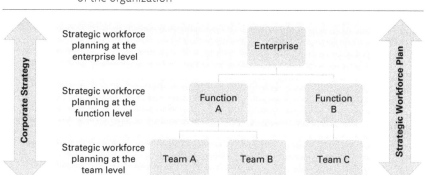

the cause and effect relationships between different functions, and how relationships across those functions must be considered holistically to develop a robust and efficient Strategic Workforce Plan. For instance, suppose our fictional company, Widgets-Are-Us, makes the decision to build a new office in Asia. One of the first considerations that must be thought out before construction of the new office can begin is how many employees will work in the office.

Regarding different functions in the organization, thinking through this example and how it could potentially impact upon the required decisions and information for those functions reveals much. One example is the facilities and real estate team, which will be dependent upon a strong Strategic Workforce Plan in order to understand building size requirements. They will also need to know how much lead time will be required to scout out a location and secure a lease, along with key planning decisions on how the office environment should look. Presumably, these teams will require detail at this level to ensure they are optimizing the space and internal environment necessary to attract and retain the talent needed for the new strategy. To this end, it is quite possible the expectations of what that office environment should look like will vary dramatically depending on the skill level and generation of the employee who ends up working in the space, which further points to the case for better planning.

More examination of the Widgets-Are-Us example reveals that finance will need to understand the Strategic Workforce Plan in order to know how much incremental headcount should be budgeted for the new office. Meanwhile, the recruiting team will need to know how many recruiters will need to be dedicated to sourcing the established incremental headcount. The HR team will require insight into the size and experience level mix of the future office employees, so they can appropriate the correct amount of support. Global mobility will need to know if there will be employees transferring to this new office and, if so, how many. The compensation, benefits and tax teams also will need to understand what the employee mix will look like in order to understand the market conditions, government regulations and tax structures required in the due diligence process. Learning and Development (L&D) will need to consider if there are any cultural implications in the training they deliver, while the IT team will need to understand technology requirements for the facility's future employees.

While not comprehensive, this example provides an illustration of how, within a typical organization, the simple strategic decision to build an office in a new location creates the need for a vast amount of people-related data and insights necessary for planning across a wide variety of functions. The more comprehensive and aligned the data and planning are on these functions in the construction and build-out of the office, the quicker the organization can turn the new location into a profitable asset.

Utilizing an SWP methodology will be useful for any role within the organization that is dependent upon or has some direct or indirect relationship with people. While people managers and decision makers in the organization tend to be the stakeholders most likely to use the insights gained from a Strategic Workforce Plan, there are additional roles that can also benefit from SWP. For example, an analyst sitting in the compensation and benefits department might require knowledge on how the changing size and demographics of an organization will impact future healthcare costs. A recruiter looking to fill a technical senior-level role could utilize SWP to understand the talent supply in the external labour market. An IT technician tasked with providing laptops and cellphones to new hires on a company's orientation day will gain insight into how many new hires will attend the orientation class each week in each location in which they are held. To that end, an onboarding coordinator will also need to know how many new hires will be starting each week to ensure the proper facilities and space are in place for the actual onboarding class.

SWP becomes exponentially more impactful to the organization when it becomes an embedded process and a mindset for the enterprise that is considered par for the course regarding how it plans and makes workforce-related decisions (Bechet, 2008). There will be more detail discussed on this topic throughout the book but, for now, just know that the basics of embedding this mindset into the organization involve realizing who, when and where it will be most effective. The more flexible organizations are regarding the who, when and where, the more the organization lends itself to developing creative solutions to workforce challenges and decisions. Furthermore, the more visibility and alignment of how different functions, teams and employees are using SWP, the more the company will benefit from the partnerships and cross-functional cooperation that will ultimately translate into a workforce that works synergistically with the broader goals and vision of that organization.

The challenges of SWP

While it is clear that the benefits of SWP to an organization have the potential to be plentiful, there are also a series of challenges that many companies face when embarking on their initial journey.

Awareness

One of the first roadblocks when attempting to build out an SWP function is creating awareness. Like introducing any new process or initiative, if there is no clear understanding of what it is and why the company is doing it, chances are it will meet resistance from both direct and indirect stakeholders. The awareness challenge can take on many forms. Some employees may simply not be clear on what the term means. Others may understand the meaning, but may not be clear on why the company has started doing it. Some may have an awareness and understanding but fail to see the real business case or upside benefit of doing it, especially given the effort that will be required.

The organization will require a solid communications strategy to roll out with the broader SWP process. Specifically, the communications strategy should address the who, what and why of SWP. There will be a deeper discussion on the positive impacts and benefits of a good communications strategy in later chapters; however, for now, just understand that a good communications strategy is beneficial because it outlines how the organization will communicate the objectives of the SWP function, when these communications will happen, how the communications will be delivered and to whom the communications will be targeted. All of this helps to create awareness and reduce the resistance to change.

Roles and responsibilities

Another potential challenge the organization could face regarding SWP is confusion regarding where the function should be situated. While it is not uncommon for SWP to be owned by HR, it is just as easy to make a case for the function or role to sit in finance, operations or even be a stand-alone 'floating' function. Wherever it does end up being positioned, it is important to remember and communicate that gaining the most value and impact will be a function of making the process a cross-functional, enterprise-wide exercise.

Data quality and quantity

A key tenet of SWP is data. Data help the SWP practitioner to understand what is happening in the workforce today, what happened yesterday and what should or could happen tomorrow. So, what is the origin of these data? It is usually safe to say that data come from a multitude of sources. One of the primary and most important sources of data, however, originates from the organization's Human Resource Information System (HRIS). Often, the challenge with many of these systems is that they are not well maintained. It is not uncommon to see incomplete or inconsistent fields in the data tables. There also can be confusion concerning data sources and definitions. In addition to these challenges, the creation of ad hoc fields is common. These ad hoc fields often require manual entries, which can lead to inconsistent or inaccurate data entries. Inconsistency in an organization's HRIS systems poses a challenge to the SWP practitioner because the use of these data can potentially lead to erroneous outputs in the analysis. Anytime an analysis with inaccurate data or erroneous results is shared with someone in the organization, there is a risk of losing credibility. A credibility hit can be particularly troublesome to the SWP practitioner trying to influence and persuade stakeholders on the value of SWP.

Scaling

It is not uncommon for organizations to begin their SWP journeys by starting with a small pilot project. Pilot projects of this nature often start in some obscure part of the organization with one or two stakeholders attempting to solve an organizational challenge. A successful pilot project can provide an epiphany of sorts to the company or department new to SWP. It can essentially act as proof of concept regarding the validity of the practice. With this small win under their belts, the organization might then make the decision to formalize a role or function in the organization that solely focuses on SWP. Once the decision has been made and plans put in place to try and replicate the success of the small pilot project at the enterprise level, the challenge of scaling begins to present itself (see Figure 1.4). The reason for this is because the complexities of SWP company-wide are much more intricate and challenging than for a smaller project where there are fewer dependent stakeholders, less data and a much smaller

Figure 1.4   Common challenges in SWP

scope. It is for this reason that it is so important for the company to have a strong vision in place for successful SWP across the enterprise. Regarding this vision, the organization should create a detailed roadmap and project plan that outlines the steps required for successful execution and implementation. Future chapters will explore the building blocks for developing an SWP roadmap in much greater detail.

Structuring an SWP function

How is a typical SWP function organized? The answer to this question is that there is no typical structure of an SWP function. Rather, the structure should depend on what the company's goals, vision and strategy are for the SWP function. To that end, tailoring the structure of an SWP team or individual to the unique circumstances of the company embarking on the journey is critical. It is important to acknowledge that the decision on how to structure the function, team or role that will own the Strategic Workforce Plan for the company should be developed as part of the upfront design. In fact, it should be one of the first questions to consider in the design phase.

Dependent upon the previously discussed goals and visions of SWP in an organization, there are many different structures that the organization could potentially pursue for its SWP function. The first one that is common in many organizations would be to have a single point of contact or individual contributor owning the entire programme. A structure of this nature is popular with organizations that have constraints around headcount (which is not uncommon) and want to start small, demonstrate proof of concept and potentially grow a team around the successes of the individual running that programme. The challenge with this approach is that it often can be difficult for a single individual alone to gain traction. Attending meetings, building relationships, influencing stakeholders and doing the analyses alone can prove to be too much. The resultant effect is the individual contributor delivering work that lacks quality and quantity.

Another possible structure is in the form of a more traditional team. A team-based approach can take on many forms. Generally speaking, there should be distinct roles and responsibilities across the team that, when brought together, provide the team with the ability to scale its impact way beyond what could be accomplished by an individual contributor alone. The structure of roles across this team should consist of a leader who works with other leaders across the organization to craft a vision, lay out a roadmap and provide leadership to ensure that vision and roadmap are commensurate with the broader organizational expectations for the function. In addition to providing leadership for the operational execution of the SWP function, the team leader should also be a subject matter expert (SME) with the requisite knowledge, skills and experience needed to work through challenges, identify opportunities and communicate progress against goals to the rest of the organization. Other key roles within the team include a statistical specialist whose primary purpose involves developing forecasts and conducting quantified statistical analysis on the current and future workforce trends. The team should also consider including a data engineer whose role would consist of writing structured query language (SQL) queries to pull and manipulate data from data warehouses. SQL is the language a data engineer uses to communicate with a database. The data engineer writes programming code for the computer that delivers a message to the database, which in turn has the database retrieving different variations and structures of data for the data engineer. SQL allows the data engineer to join and merge disparate data sources together to create new data tables along with developing dashboards for the tracking of metrics. Finally, the team should have an insights partner whose role involves working directly with stakeholders across the business. Their primary goal would be to better understand business requirements, strategic drivers and future organizational trends and objectives. The insights partner will also work with these same stakeholders to communicate the results of analyses, along with providing consulting support in the form of recommendations. Regarding the insights role, the organization might want to include project management as being in the scope of activities for this role. Alternatively, the company could have a stand-alone project manager whose role would include typical project management activities, such as scheduling and leading meetings, developing and owning project artefacts and tracking project deliverables and activities. Ideally, the project manager would also own the change management and communications plans.

The size of an SWP team is once again dependent upon the ultimate vision and impact the organization hopes to derive from this team. That said, the larger and more matrixed the organization, the more complicated it becomes to deliver on an enterprise-wide Strategic Workforce Plan. It is at this inflection point that large global companies need to consider the SWP function in the context of either a centralized or decentralized approach. Before deciding upon either of these approaches, however, the organization should reflect on some key questions, such as:

- Should there be regional teams?
- Should the function organize teams by business units and, if so, what should be the size of these teams?
- Should the function develop a centralized centre of excellence?
- Should the function have in-person support at every site?
- Finally, where should the function be based?

On the final question, it is not uncommon to have questions regarding which function or part of the organization an SWP team should sit within to have maximum impact. In the more traditional model, SWP teams sit in HR, but there is also a solid case for having these teams sit in finance or operations. Team location once again becomes a question of end vision, strategy, organizational competencies and broader enterprise-wide organizational design.

Jobs, roles and skills in the SWP process

Consideration of the different types of roles required for an optimal Strategic Workforce Plan was touched on in the previous section. While this is a good place to begin, there is more to consider than just the types of roles within the team. More important than the roles themselves are the skill sets and competencies that the employees who are in those roles possess. While there will be an entire chapter dedicated to this topic later in the book (Chapter 7), it is still worth mentioning the importance of this topic as part of the introduction to SWP.

Developing the criteria for the skills and competencies that an SWP team requires for success is once again dependent upon many factors, such as the goals and vision for SWP in the organization, the industry within which that organization operates and the availability of talent with regards to office and company location. These factors aside, there are certain must-haves when it comes to skill sets for an SWP team to possess for maximum impact. Furthermore, depending upon the role in the team, those skills can vary widely. The following list provides a good starting point when considering the unique skill sets that an individual should possess in the roles that were discussed earlier in this chapter.

Team leader

- leadership experience;
- executive presence;
- communication skills;
- ability to influence;
- negotiation skills;
- analytical mindset;
- attention to detail;
- SWP and analytics experience;
- storytelling with data;
- project management;
- ability to work under pressure;
- problem solving;
- creativity.

It is clear from this list that the characteristics an SWP leader should possess are like the leadership qualities that would be considered desirable in any leadership position. The primary difference is the actual background in more specialized skills like analytics, SWP and project management.

Data engineer

- database administration;
- SQL language;

- Python;
- R;
- SQL;
- Excel;
- statistics;
- ability to ask the right questions;
- ability to work under pressure;
- ability to break down complex problems into manageable outputs that are easy to explain.

The skill sets essential from the team's data engineer are deeply rooted in database administration with the ability to write complex SQL queries. Individuals in this role must be able to merge and join disparate data sets and have the ability to communicate the methodology and approach that was used to create these data sets. These individuals must also be able to work under pressure and have the ability to manage competing priorities.

Insights partner

- consulting background;
- communication skills;
- analytical skills;
- data visualization;
- storytelling with data;
- project management;
- change management;
- meeting effectiveness;
- managing competing priorities.

Many of the skills that the insights partner possesses are similar to the team leader. The biggest differences are that the insights partner will not require the same level of executive presence and influence as the team leader. The insights partner role should serve as a confidant to the external stakeholders. Project management and managing change and communications plans will be a big part of this role.

Analytics specialist

- data modelling;
- statistics;
- SQL;
- R;
- forecasting;
- data curiosity;
- data visualization;
- data creativity;
- highly analytical;
- abstract thinking;
- ability to communicate methodology and statistical findings in layman's terms;
- ability to manage competing priorities.

The analytics specialist should be considered to be the team's quantitative expert. This role should not be confused with the data engineer role, where the focus is more specifically on pulling reports from the HRIS, manipulating data and building dashboards. The analytics specialist, in contrast, is a role that provides the team with the majority of the statistical analysis. Daily activities might include creating statistical forecasts, inferential studies and predictive analytics.

Summary of chapter objectives

SWP and its practical application for companies and organizations

SWP is the process of thinking through the challenges and opportunities that an organization's people could/will face as market conditions change and business cycles mature. It seeks to define how the organization's workforce structure should evolve as these market conditions change and the business develops. Simply put, SWP is the function within a company tasked with identifying people-related opportunities and challenges associated with changes to the business and then developing a plan to capitalize on the opportunities and mitigate the risks linked to those challenges. SWP is a process that can be leveraged across the entire organization to improve performance. It gives managers in all functions across the business a set of tools to assess and improve their team's performance by being proactive in how they plan for the future.

The purpose and benefits of SWP

The purpose of SWP is to improve the performance of the company or organization. Improving the organization's performance through its people can be achieved by better alignment of skills, programmes, teams and day-to-day work with the strategy, objectives and goals of that company or organization. SWP benefits the organization because it provides managers, leaders and HR professionals with insights regarding the current and future state of the workforce. Workforce insights of this nature provide these managers, leaders and HR professionals with the information they need to make optimal workforce-related decisions. Having the knowledge and ability to make the best decisions for the organization's workforce in turn will lead to cost-effectiveness, efficiency gains and performance improvement for the organization.

SWP is also a mechanism for bridging the gap between the organization's corporate strategy and its workforce strategy. Aligning corporate and workforce strategies is crucial for maximizing future company performance. This is because so much of the corporate strategy is dependent on having a workforce in place that has the talent necessary to execute on the strategy's objectives. Developing a workforce with this talent begins with alignment of the workforce and corporate strategies, which is exactly what SWP helps the organization to do.

The challenges of SWP

Change management and communications plans are essential parts of any SWP programme. The likelihood of facing resistance when first embarking on a journey into SWP is high. Practitioners should be prepared to defend the business case behind creating a Strategic Workforce Plan and/or team. In addition to having strong change management and communications structures in place, executive support is crucial for scaling the programme and gaining credibility across the organization.

Structuring of an SWP function

There are many possible team structures that can be implemented in building out an SWP function. Structures can range from a one-person team to a fully built-out matrixed function that spans across regions and business units. The structure of the SWP function is largely dependent on the goals, mission and vision for the programme within the individual business.

Outlining key jobs, roles and skills involved in SWP

Independent of the structure of the SWP team are the skill sets required for optimal impact. These skills are largely a function of the goals, mission and vision for the team, but there are certain skills that should be included in any SWP programme. These skills can be thought of in terms of soft (non-technical) and hard (technical) skills and include but are not limited to those listed in Table 1.1.

Table 1.1 Common challenges in SWP

Soft skills	Hard skills
Leadership experience	Data modelling
Executive presence	Statistics
Communication skills	SQL
Ability to influence	R
Negotiation skills	Forecasting
Attention to detail	Data curiosity
Project management	Data visualization
Ability to work under pressure	Data creativity
Problem solving	Analytical skills
Creativity	Storytelling with data
Change management	Project management
Meeting effectiveness	
Communication skills	
Prioritization skills	

Aligning workforce and corporate strategies

02

CHAPTER OBJECTIVES

1 Define workforce strategy.

2 Define corporate strategy.

3 List the factors that can affect a workforce strategy.

4 Outline key activities involved in bringing corporate and workforce strategies together.

Workforce strategy

As illustrated in Figure 2.1, a workforce strategy is a combination of the vision, goals and decisions that an organization makes with regards to its employees. This type of strategy can take on many forms. It can be short term or long term. It can be something as simple as deciding how many new employees will be hired or as complicated as making strategic decisions on a multitude of factors such as hiring, retention, engagement or training, just to name a few (Huselid, Becker and Beatty, 2005).

The key elements that distinguish a workforce strategy are the fact that a) a workforce strategy includes definitive and measurable goals; and b) a workforce strategy outlines a defined timeline and key actions required for the achievement of those goals (Huselid, Becker and Beatty, 2005). The difference between a good and bad workforce

Figure 2.1 Foundations of a workforce strategy

strategy usually equates to the amount of upfront time and thought that has been put into that strategy. In addition to being detailed and well thought-out, good workforce strategies have an equally well-defined and thought-out plan to execute in conjunction with the strategy. Good workforce strategies are effectively able to communicate what the end goal is, the purpose of accomplishing that goal and a plan that outlines the actions to achieve the goal.

In contrast, an inadequate workforce strategy is one that is not a strategy at all, but rather a series of actions or events that are at work with no end goal in sight and no clear link to an outcome that will support positive business performance. An example of this would be an organization making the decision to hire 100 new welders purely on the basis that they hired 100 new welders the year before. Conversely, if the purpose of hiring those welders is to support a new manufacturing plant in Western Canada, and that manufacturing facility is expanding its capabilities to manufacture a new product, where that new product is part of an expansion into a whole new market to support company growth, it is easy to see what the purpose of hiring those welders is and how the end goal links to a broader organizational strategy.

The challenge that many organizations run into with workforce strategies is that the notion of formalized policies of this nature can sometimes be a foreign concept in the context of how they approach current processes and business strategies. They may already be developing and executing on workforce strategies, but may not have formally acknowledged that they are doing so. The danger with this is that it can lead to the organization going into autopilot mode when it comes to workforce-related decisions. When autopilot mode does manifest itself, the requirement of spending upfront time defining and ultimately making decisions can sometimes go by the wayside, which for obvious reasons leads to suboptimal decision making.

Corporate strategy

A corporate strategy consists of the activities, policies and decisions that an organization takes to increase its shareholder value. While this is a relatively broad definition, it is important to understand the role of corporate strategy in the context of developing a workforce strategy. That is to say, whether directly or indirectly, the workforce can play a fundamental role in developing value for a company (Ansoff and McDonnell, 1988). Before diving deeper into the relationship between the corporate and workforce strategy, however, it is important to have more context on what a corporate strategy is.

The corporate strategy consists of a series of strategic pillars (see Figure 2.2) that, when combined, set the tone for how the organization will create long-term value. It is important to note that these distinct aspects of corporate strategy ultimately begin with the organization's mission, vision and broader business model. These key pillars consist of:

1 The long-term direction the company chooses to pursue.

2 The depth and breadth of the scope of activities the organization will pursue with regards to its long-term strategy.

3 How the organization will position itself among its competitors.

4 How the organization positions itself within its particular industry.

5 How the organization will use its resources to add value.

6 The organization's culture.

Figure 2.2   Corporate strategy pillars

Long-Term Vision
Scope of Activities
Resources
Competitive Positioning
Organizational Culture

Long-term vision

The long-term vision is the component of the corporate strategy that sets the tone for the remaining aspects. It asks the question: where are we today and where do we want to be tomorrow? Developing a long-term vision involves having a strong understanding of the organization's industry, its core competencies and its competitors. It also requires understanding both micro and macroeconomic trends that have the potential to impact the business environment in which it operates.

Scope of activities

In addition to thinking through the vision for the company, there are also decisions that require thought and planning regarding the scope of activities the company will adopt to execute on that vision. These questions might include:

- How many products or services will the organization develop?
- In what regions will the organization operate?
- Will the organization compete in one or multiple industries?
- Will products be branded under one or multiple names?

Competitive positioning

How a company competes with competitors is a fundamental aspect of any corporate strategy. There are various tactics a company can choose when thinking through its competitor strategy. Among these, a company might decide to compete on price, which equates to being a low-cost provider. Conversely, it might compete on quality and exclusivity (think Rolls-Royce versus Kia), in which case price is likely to be higher. Advertising campaigns and brand reputation are other areas in which a company can compete. Businesses like Coca-Cola and Disney have done an excellent job of building their brand equity. Regarding this approach, whatever the company does decide to compete on, there should be careful consideration put into the necessary decisions and the trade-offs between risk versus reward for that competitive positioning decision. It is in evaluating these trade-offs that the strategy component of competitive positioning plays a significant role.

Resources

Thinking through the organization's resources and how they can best be leveraged to support the rest of the corporate strategy, in itself, is a huge part of that strategy. Think of a company's resources as the composition of technology, equipment, skills and workforce used to create value in the organization's day-to-day activities. It is in this aspect of corporate strategy where we see a high-level need to have a reliable workforce strategy. This will be discussed more later in this chapter, but for now know that it can represent the difference between an organization's ability to execute or not on the daily tasks required to realize longer-term value.

Organizational culture

The culture of an organization is the final component that needs consideration when developing a corporate strategy. Organizational culture refers to how the company operates and defines itself internally. According to Needle (2010), organizational culture represents the collective values, beliefs and principles of organizational members. Is there a strict dress code enforced or are employees allowed to dress casually? Does everyone show up to the office late and work late, or does everyone work from home? Does the company place great emphasis on ethics and social responsibility or is increasing profit margins the only objective the company considers to be a priority. Questions like these, which may seem inconsequential, go a long way towards developing the DNA of a company. Providing the right answers to these issues is crucial in establishing the foundation for a long and prosperous organizational life cycle. Companies like General Electric, which have been around for many decades, provide excellent examples of the importance of building a healthy corporate culture. On the opposite end of the spectrum, the cataclysmic failure of companies such as Enron and WorldCom are stark reminders of the very real consequences that a toxic corporate culture can create.

Factors that can affect a workforce strategy

Various factors have the potential to impact the direction of a workforce strategy. Within these factors, however, are three distinct categories that tend to stand out as being especially important. These three categories include the labour market, current and future technology and the organization's corporate strategy (see Figure 2.3).

Figure 2.3   Key factors that affect a workforce strategy

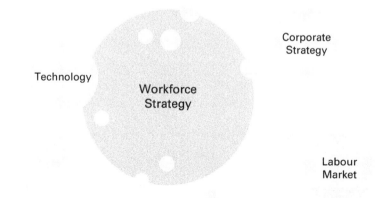

Corporate
Strategy

Technology

Workforce
Strategy

Labour
Market

Labour market

The labour market is a major factor that needs consideration when developing a workforce strategy. The reason for this is simple: the labour market is the starting point for the supply of talent required to build out the workforce strategy. Not surprisingly, this becomes one of the largest dependencies in the construction of a workforce strategy. Which is to say, without a reliable source to supply talent to the workforce, it becomes difficult to develop a reliable workforce strategy. Understanding the relationship between the skills and job profiles required to build out a workforce strategy and the availability and location of those skills and job profiles becomes paramount when determining the organization's ability to develop a comprehensive workforce strategy. Answers to questions such as the following are needed:

- Are the skills required for the organization's workforce strategy ubiquitous or very specialized and in limited supply?
- Are there 'pockets' of these skills concentrated in certain regions or are they distributed evenly around the world?
- Do the skills in question require ongoing training and certification or are they static once achieved?
- Will the skill requirements change over time or be dependent upon new technologies?
- Is compensation for the skills uniform around the globe or is there an opportunity for geographical arbitrage?
- Do the skills require a university education and, if so, how does the trend in graduation rates look?
- Do graduation rates vary by location and region?
- Are there certain profiles that tend to be present in candidates that possess these skills? For example, are they mobile?

Providing answers to these questions will help to supply business and HR leaders with the insight necessary to build a workforce strategy that reflects the realities of the environment in which the organization operates.

Current and future technology

Technology is another factor for consideration when thinking through the components to include in a workforce strategy. To understand how technology could impact a workforce strategy, consider two technological components that touch the workforce. The first is the technology that employees in the organization use to perform their day-to-day activities, eg a basic laptop. The second is the role of technology in the organization relating to the service and products that are delivered and developed.

Regarding the first component, it is important to understand how advances in technology might impact the skills required to use the technology in daily activities. For example, suppose modern organizations never adjusted their skill requirements from proficiency on typewriters to proficiency on computers. It is safe to say that it probably would have faced a significant headwind in trying to keep up with competitors that possessed a workforce full of employees who did possess these skills.

The second component deals with how future developments in technology might change and even make redundant the general day-to-day work and tasks that employees perform on a regular basis. Machine learning (ML) and advances in artificial intelligence (AI) and robotics are already changing the way in which companies work. There will be much more detailed discussion on this topic in the coming chapters, but suffice it to say that a good workforce strategy should factor in some of these technological advances and consider how they are poised to change the structure and philosophy behind how organizations work.

Corporate performance indicators and their relationship to the workforce

Whether implicitly or explicitly acknowledged, most organizations have key performance indicators (KPIs) that help to measure the performance of different aspects of their organization (Parmenter, 2015). KPIs can vary significantly depending on the industry and business in question but, even across this variance, there are a few KPIs that most companies track with some level of interest. A broad example might be revenue earned per quarter. Intuitively, the reason why this is important is that, without revenue, the company would not be able to pay expenses and grow the business. KPIs or 'business drivers' are especially useful when going through the exercises of developing a Strategic Workforce Plan and creating a workforce strategy because, when understood and used correctly, they help to provide a quantifiable business measure to assess the current and future state of the workforce.

To illustrate this point with a simplified example, assume a fictional company tracks and measures both monthly revenue and headcount growth. Here we can see that, based on market trends, new product offerings and pricing strategies, the company has developed a three-year revenue forecast. Because the company has tracked monthly headcount in tandem with its revenue growth, a relationship can be established between revenue and headcount growth (if a relationship exists). Understanding this relationship is powerful in the context of SWP because it provides the SWP practitioner with a quantified, business-driven metric to use in the development of future headcount requirements. While this example is oversimplified, it does illustrate why understanding business drivers is so important in SWP. These drivers are the first step in aligning the workforce strategy with the broader business strategy.

Merging workforce and corporate strategies together

A theme that will appear throughout this book is the notion of aligning workforce strategy with corporate strategy. Alignment of the two is necessary because creating workforce strategies and Strategic Workforce Plans in tandem with the organization's corporate strategy creates significantly more value to the organization than creating these plans and strategies in a silo (Gubman, 1998). It is for this reason that historically the HR function has not been thought of as a partner in creating the same level of value throughout the enterprise as more traditional functions like marketing and R&D. With the proper framework, cross-functional partnerships and executive support, however, the HR function is in a prime position to add as much value or more than other functions in the organization.

The first step in bringing corporate and workforce strategies together is the acknowledgement and agreement across the business that, through proper planning, HR can add value and, in turn, should be a significant component of the broader corporate planning process. Once consensus has been reached on HR's role in the corporate strategy planning process, it is up to the HR function to outline how it will add this value. HR can do this by focusing on three key areas: the current state of the workforce, the future state of the workforce and the business drivers mentioned earlier in this chapter.

The current state of the workforce

In this step of the process, the SWP practitioner should be looking to understand the present structure of the workforce. Essentially the question here is: how is the workforce distributed? Specific questions that should be asked when assessing this current state include:

- What is the size of the current workforce?
- What are the key roles in the workforce and how do they support the broader business?
- What are the demographic trends in age and experience level of the workforce?
- Where is the workforce located?
- What is the ratio of full-time employees (FTEs) to contractors and contingent workers?

Answering these questions will provide the baseline data required to understand how the organization's workforce currently supports the company in achieving its strategic goals. Also, answering these questions will give insight into what requirements can be expected of the workforce to support the corporate strategy in the future.

The future state of the workforce

The questions that require answering in this step of the process will build from the questions and analysis completed when understanding the current state of the workforce. The difference in this step of the process is that the requirements that will inform the workforce strategy should be fully dependent upon the future corporate strategy. It is here that the cross-functional partnership becomes so important. The questions regarding scope for this part of the analysis will be similar to the last section, but focused more specifically on how changes in future aspects of the corporate strategy could potentially change the mix in the workforce distribution discussed earlier.

The framing of questions in this part of the process should be more along the lines of: if the company is planning to launch a new product that it will be manufacturing offshore, what are the implications of this decision on the current location of its employees? Alternatively, if the company is planning a significant expansion into a new market in Asia, how will this impact headcount growth, recruiting and space planning? It is easy to see that the questions asked and answered in this part of the process are much more dependent on specific aspects of the future direction of the corporate strategy. It should be noted, however, that these questions cannot be adequately answered without first understanding the current distribution of the workforce.

Business drivers

Understanding and defining the relationship between the main business drivers and their impact on the distribution of the workforce is the final component that the HR and SWP teams should be prepared to analyse and present during the broader corporate strategy discussions. It is the strength of the relationship between these business drivers and the current and future workforce requirements that will inform many of the decisions regarding the development and execution of a workforce strategy and Strategic Workforce Plan.

This step of the strategy development phase requires the need for more statistically driven and quantified analyses. One of the best methods to help understand the strength of the relationship between business drivers and headcount requirements is through a linear regression analysis. Testing the hypothesis that a certain business driver has a strong relationship with an outcome variable like head-count can be proven or disproven through the regression technique. Establishing relationships between the business drivers is important because the entire concept of aligning workforce strategy with corporate strategy is predicated on the notion that a cause and effect relationship exists between the two. In other words, if we know that there is a relationship between budgeted R&D spend and the number of engineers required in the R&D division, we can then derive the correct number of engineers to hire for this division when corporate strategy calls for a doubling of the R&D budget.

Summary of chapter objectives

Workforce strategy

A workforce strategy is the starting point for developing a Strategic Workforce Plan. When done properly, a workforce strategy should be a component of the broader corporate strategy. One of the keys to developing a reliable workforce strategy is ensuring the KPIs of the organization are in sync with workforce-related outcomes. Ensuring the existence of a stable relationship between the two provides the SWP practitioner with a method of quantifying and optimizing future workforce requirements based on the strategic direction of the company.

Corporate strategy

A corporate strategy consists of the activities, policies and decisions that an organization utilizes to increase its shareholder value. The corporate strategy consists of a series of strategic pillars that, when combined, set the tone for how the organization will create long-term value. It is important to note that these distinct aspects of corporate strategy ultimately begin with the organization's mission, vision and broader business model. These key pillars consist of:

1 The long-term direction that the company chooses to pursue.

2 The depth and breadth of the scope of activities the organization will pursue with regards to its long-term strategy.

3 How the organization will position itself among its competitors.

4 How the organization positions itself within its particular industry.

5 How the organization will use its resources to add value.

6 The organization's culture.

Factors that can affect a workforce strategy

In addition to understanding the corporate strategy, it is important to understand internal and external factors that have the potential to impact the workforce strategy. Key considerations that have the ability to affect a workforce strategy include:

- the labour market;
- current technology;
- future technology;
- corporate strategy decisions.

Merging workforce and corporate strategies together

Developing workforce strategies and Strategic Workforce Plans in tandem with the organization's corporate strategy creates significantly more value to the organization than creating these plans and strategies in silos. There are some key factors that should be considered when merging workforce and corporate strategies together, including:

- the current state of the workforce;
- the future state of the workforce;
- key business drivers and performance indicators.

As it relates to HR contributing to corporate strategy discussions, when the HR and SWP teams focus on understanding the current and future state of the workforce along with the company's KPIs, the opportunity and likelihood for adding value through participation in these discussions increases significantly.

Conclusion

This chapter has discussed the role of workforce strategy in SWP. Workforce strategy is an important concept to understand in SWP because it is essentially the foundation for turning a workforce strategy into a plan of action for utilizing the workforce as a lever to increase organizational performance. The focus of the next several chapters now will shift from understanding SWP and workforce strategy to better understanding some of the fundamental aspects of creating a robust Strategic Workforce Plan.

Understanding workforce demand

03

CHAPTER OBJECTIVES

1 Define workforce demand.
2 Explore the factors that can affect workforce demand.
3 Explore the factors that need to be considered before using workforce demand in a Strategic Workforce Plan.

Workforce demand

Workforce or labour demand refers to the internal and external demand for skills, experience and education that companies need to accomplish their primary mission, goals and strategy. Hamermesh (1996) defines labour demand as any decision made by an employer regarding the company's workers, their employment, their compensation and their training. As it relates to SWP, it is important to understand workforce demand because doing so can reveal if there are any gaps in the demand versus the current supply of said skills, experience and education (see Figure 3.1). In the context of a Strategic Workforce Plan, analysing this demand can show trends that may reveal an excess or shortage of these skills, experience and education. Incorporating these factors into the workforce strategy and Strategic Workforce Plan will support the goal of a more optimized workforce.

It is important to note that, from an employee standpoint, workforce demand can mean different things. For instance, it might refer to the specific skills an employee has, or it can refer to the education or

Figure 3.1　Elements of workforce demand

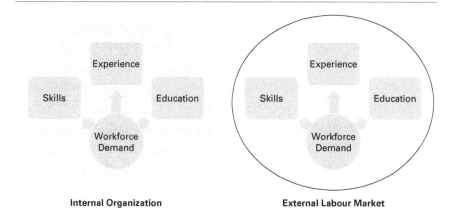

Internal Organization　　　　　　External Labour Market

experience level that employee possesses. Because workforce demand does encompass different dimensions, the organization should go through the process of defining how it will categorize these dimensions. Why is this component critical? Because when the time comes to formalize the workforce strategy, which will inevitably involve a sourcing plan, the talent acquisition team will need a detailed outline of the candidates they will have to source. For example, suppose a recruiter is told to recruit 20 software engineers. Some initial questions they might have include:

- What specific coding skills should they possess, eg Java, C++ or Python?
- Should these software engineers be junior or senior or a mix of both?
- Is there a particular educational background they should possess?

Internal demand

Put simply, internal demand is the total volume or number of employees, skills, experience level or education required by the company to operate efficiently and to achieve its organizational objectives. Workforce demand includes both the current workers needed to complete day-to-day tasks and the workers that might not currently be in the organization but will be required for future projects or work.

Understanding internal demand is a critical component in developing a successful and useful workforce strategy and Strategic Workforce Plan. It is the foundation for gaining insight into whether or not there will be an increase or decrease in employees or skills required by the organization in the future. One might be inclined to ask how workforce demand lends itself to assisting in the understanding of future employees and expertise needed by the company. The answer lies in the link between internal business drivers (discussed in the last chapter) and the organization's people. When correlated to the company's headcount and skills requirements, these drivers become anchors for understanding the workforce support required for the future and, as such, form an integral part of the SWP process.

The method of defining internal demand is composed of two parts. The first part is understanding the current state of workforce demand. To some degree, current workforce demand is similar to current workforce supply. The primary difference between the two, however, stems from the fact that, although an employee might be working in a particular role with a specific set of skills, this does not necessarily equate to there being a demand for those skills. Why? Because organizational strategies change and so do the skills and employees required to execute on those strategies. The role and the skills that are foundational in particular jobs may no longer be relevant in the organization. As it relates to understanding the current workforce demand, the SWP practitioner is essentially doing an inventory of the workforce to understand which positions and skills are currently in demand and which ones are not. Once this is complete, they can then use the Strategic Workforce Plan as a medium for optimizing those skills and jobs to create a workforce strategy that is more future looking and supportive of the organization's corporate strategy.

The second component of future workforce demand centres around learning what skills, jobs and employees will be required as the company's strategy evolves. Gaining insight into the future skills and roles that match the requirements of the organization's strategy involves building a strong partnership between HR, the SWP team (or individual) and business leaders. More specifically, the SWP practitioner needs to understand how the internal demand for certain roles and skills will change over time so they can identify the appropriate business drivers to correlate with this future demand. Doing so ultimately will lead to developing an aligned and practical forecast to assist in the development of the workforce strategy and Strategic Workforce Plan.

External demand

External demand is similar to internal demand but, as the name implies, focuses on external rather than internal factors. Think of external demand as being the summation of demand for all skills or jobs by all the businesses and organizations competing for those skills and jobs across all industries and sectors. To that point, it is important to note that external demand is not specific to the particular industry in which a company competes, rather it refers to the total demand across all sectors and industries around the world.

Factoring external workforce demand into a Strategic Workforce Plan is critical because it is the starting point for understanding how much competition there is for the skills and jobs around the world region, country and site location. Accurately assessing the external demand for these skills and jobs is crucial in order to answer questions such as the following:

- Is demand for the organization's critical expertise and jobs increasing, decreasing or remaining the same in the external labour market?
- Is the demand for these skills concentrated in a particular industry or are changes in demand being felt across the entire sector?
- Are there locations where demand is higher or is demand steady across the globe?
- Is there a trend for more or less demand for these skills and jobs in the external labour market?
- Is increased demand driving up the cost of labour for these skills and jobs?
- Are there new technologies that have the potential to impact future demand?
- Are there any trends in university graduation rates for specific degree programmes that can be leading indicators of changes in workforce demand?

With answers to these questions in place, the SWP practitioner can ensure the Strategic Workforce Plan includes the necessary actions to mitigate against the risk posed by potential threats from the market related to this demand. Answering these questions also can provide insight into opportunities to optimize recruitment and talent strategies that place the organization in a more offensive position regarding any impending 'talent wars' with industry competitors.

Factors that can affect workforce demand

A critical component of understanding workforce demand is possessing knowledge around the factors that can impact that demand. Insight into these factors involves thinking through how workforce demand could be affected across four different dimensions, which are:

- short-term external demand;
- long-term external demand;
- short-term internal demand;
- long-term internal demand.

The SWP practitioner needs to think through the factors that could affect workforce demand from both a short/long-term perspective and an internal/external perspective.

Short-term external demand

As discussed earlier in this chapter, external demand refers to the demand for skills and jobs by direct or indirect competitors across industries and sectors. The short-term component of external demand usually relates to a zero to three-year timeframe. The factors that have the potential to impact workforce demand in the short term are typically related to major capital projects that competitors in the relevant talent market might be involved in. For clarity, a capital project is a significant investment by a company to improve infrastructure, increase market share, launch a new project or expand into a new region or country (Merrett and Sykes, 1973). The reason these capital projects have the potential to affect workforce demand is that they often involve a substantial upfront investment in skills and labour which the organization requires to complete the project. The size and scope of some capital projects can be so significant that the upfront requirement for these skills and labour can change the demand dynamic in the job market. It becomes necessary then for the SWP practitioner always to be evaluating the job market for any news that would suggest a major capital project is on the horizon.

Long-term external demand

Compared to short-term external demand where the focus is typically on a three-year time span, long-term demand looks past three years. Also, the factors that affect workforce demand in the long run tend to be more technologically focused compared to shorter-term demand. When considering this form of workforce demand, it is crucial to think about the cause-and-effect relationships between technological breakthroughs and this demand. The reason for this is because, when a breakthrough does happen, it can lead to an increase in demand for one skill set along with an equal decrease in demand for another skill set (this is mainly because the new technology may have rendered the original skill set redundant). One need look no further than the transportation sector over the last 100 years to see how technological advances can impact the skills required to stay competitive. From horse-drawn carriages to self-driving vehicles, the transportation industry is a good example of the importance of monitoring new technologies and understanding the potential impact that these changes can have on the demand for workers.

Short-term internal demand

At 18 months, short-term internal demand has an even shorter timeframe than short-term external demand. Workforce demand of this nature relates to the incremental headcount companies budget for during their budgeting process. Like short-term external demand, this sort of demand also tends to be in reaction to new projects; however, it can also include demand due to attrition in the form of backfill and steady state growth. The factors that can impact short-term demand include new projects, backfill from attrition and headcount that was under-budgeted from the prior year (this is usually a function of improper SWP).

The biggest challenge regarding short-term internal demand is understanding if the demand is real or merely a function of hiring managers turning true demand into an over-inflated wish list used to foster excess capacity to support their team's agendas. This 'head-count padding' is another example of the need to ensure a quantitative approach is used to calculate real demand. This is a reoccurring theme which will be discussed later in this chapter and throughout the book.

Long-term internal demand

Not surprisingly, the factors that affect long-term demand are less apparent compared to other dimensions of workforce demand. The reason for this is simply because the further the organization looks into the future, the more uncertainty there is. Although the future may be uncertain, this is no excuse to ignore the factors that have the potential to impact future demand. Those factors tend to mirror broader macroeconomic trends in the economy. What this means is the health of the economy tends to be one of the strongest indicators of longer-term external demand. Moreover, when the economy is booming, organizations tend to be more aggressive with growth and expansion plans, which leads to more demand for labour and skills. Conversely, when the economy is in a retraction or recession, companies tend to tighten up their spending and even scale down their workforce, leading to a significant reduction in demand for labour and skills. It is for this reason that the SWP practitioner needs to continually monitor key economic indicators and stay in tune with trends in the macroeconomic environment.

Future technologies, which have been a discussion point throughout this chapter, comprise another factor that stands to have a significant impact on future workforce demand. These technologies are either in their infancy but do exist today or are ideas that have yet to make it to the market. The SWP practitioner should remain apprised of the latest industry trends and touch base with their company's R&D

teams to ensure they have a firm grasp of projects in their pipeline from a new technologies perspective. While it can be challenging to develop plans or immediate actions to address these future technologies, it is still worth acknowledging them and engaging in dialogues and high-level plans for what the organization might do if these technologies transpire into reality.

Factors to consider when incorporating workforce demand into a Strategic Workforce Plan

While this chapter has briefly touched upon some of the factors to consider when determining workforce demand, taking these separate components and piecing them together to form a broader strategy is where the real added value happens. As illustrated in Figure 3.2, the formulation of this strategy involves several key elements: macroeconomic factors, industry assessment and corporate strategy objectives.

Macroeconomic factors

Factoring the macroeconomic environment into the equation for assessing and incorporating workforce demand into the workforce strategy is crucial. The first step of this process involves brainstorming macroeconomic factors that could potentially impact future workforce demand. This exercise tends to be most useful when done in tandem or as a partnership with the organization's HR and business leaders.

A practical approach for brainstorming is to gather a group of six to eight cross-functional leaders in a room. On a whiteboard, write out three themes entitled: *past macroeconomic variables*, *current economic variables* and *future economic variables*. Next, provide group participants with sticky notes and have them write and categorize their applicable ideas for macroeconomic variables under each of the categories. It is important to ensure that the brainstorming participants understand the purpose of the exercise and fully grasp the concept and characteristics that encompass macroeconomic variables.

Figure 3.2 Incorporating workforce demand into the Strategic Workforce Plan

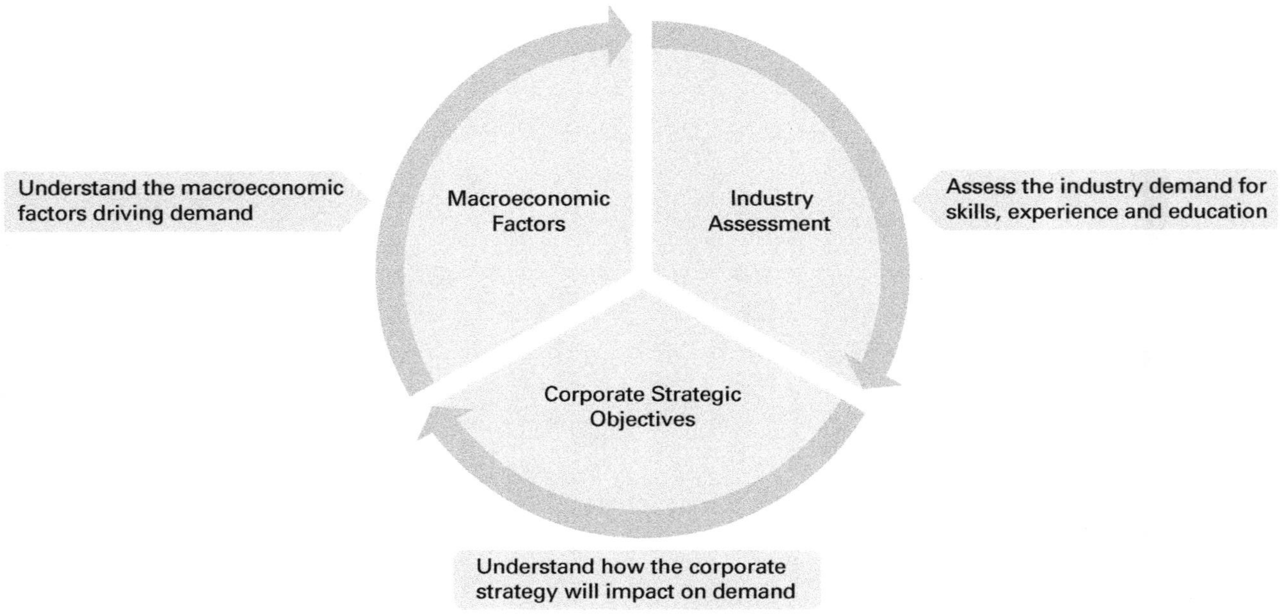

Once the group participants have included their inputs under each category, finalize the activity by further categorizing those results into subcategories that capture common macroeconomic factors arising from the participants' contributions. Ideally, this will lead to four or five key themes for consideration in the broader workforce demand strategy.

Conducting an industry assessment

The next component that should be analysed and included in the workforce demand strategy involves assessing the impact of the organization's industry on the current and future demand for skills and employees. Examining the impact of industry trends on the organization's workforce demand can be accomplished by utilizing the previously identified macroeconomic variables. What this equates to is taking those variables and applying them through the lens of the specific industry the organization competes within. Typically this will lead to a series of questions that should be asked and answered. Example questions include the following:

- Is the industry the organization competes within growing, retracting or remaining static?

- Is the industry the organization competes within dispersed globally or centric to a particular region in the world (eg technology in Silicon Valley)?

- What percentage of total gross domestic product (GDP) does the organization's industry contribute?

- Is the industry's share of GDP increasing or decreasing?

- Is the organization's industry seasonal or cyclical?

- What does the average life cycle look like in the organization's industry?

Incorporating corporate strategic objectives

The final step of the workforce demand strategy centres around incorporating and transforming the corporate strategy into critical demand drivers that have the potential to impact future internal demand. As discussed earlier in this chapter, this translates into gaining insight into the relationship between the primary business drivers and the current and future requirements for skills and jobs. It is critical that this component of the demand strategy be worked through in tandem with the organization's business leaders. While it is possible for the SWP practitioner to complete the exercise without input from these leaders, a more cross-functional partnership approach will lead to more robust and practical metrics. Partnering with business leaders will also strengthen the relationship between the SWP function and the rest of the business and reduce the amount of resistance to the fully developed workforce strategy and accompanying Strategic Workforce Plan.

The formulated workforce demand strategy

With these three steps completed, the SWP practitioner should have in their possession a workforce demand strategy that takes into account internal and external factors, the company's corporate strategy and a risk mitigation component. A holistic approach to demand planning, such as the one outlined in this chapter, will help to ensure the organization not only has contingencies in place for unforeseen events, but also has a strategy in place to take advantage of opportunities to compete better using its talents.

Summary of chapter objectives

Defining workforce demand

Workforce demand refers to the summation of skills, experience and education that organizations require to accomplish the work necessary to execute on their broader business models and strategic objectives. It is essential for the SWP practitioner to acknowledge the fact that workforce demand comes in two forms: internal demand and external demand.

Internal demand refers to the short and long-term demand for skills, experience and education that the organization requires to accomplish its core goals and strategy. This internal demand includes the incremental demand for these skills, experience and education, as well as the current existence of skills, experience and education in the organization. To that end, it is crucial to note that, just because there is some form of skills, experience and education in the organization, this does not translate into actual demand for those skills, experience and education. Put simply, it is possible that these skills, experience and education once may have been in demand but, due to changes in the organization's strategy, may no longer be required. This is why it is important for the SWP practitioner to continually go through the process of evaluating the organization's current distribution of those skills, experience and education.

External demand, on the other hand, refers to those same skills, experience and education, but on an aggregate (global and regional) level. It can be useful to think of external demand as the demand for the entire universe of skills, experience and education across all sectors, industries and competitors. External demand is one of the primary reasons why it is important to have a solid grasp of the macro-economic factors that can affect workforce demand. Why? Because these factors tend to be leading indicators of variables impacting that universe of skills, experience and education.

Factors that can affect workforce demand

A critical component of understanding workforce demand is possessing knowledge around what the factors are that stand to impact demand. Insight into these factors involves thinking through how workforce demand could be affected across four different dimensions, which are: short-term external demand, long-term external demand, short-term internal demand and long-term internal demand. The SWP practitioner needs to think through the factors that could affect workforce demand from both a short/long-term perspective and an internal/external perspective.

Using workforce demand in a Strategic Workforce Plan

Finally, when developing a workforce demand strategy to incorporate into the broader workforce strategy and accompanying Strategic Workforce Plan, a sensible approach is to break down the three primary factors of workforce demand planning into separate components. These factors include: macroeconomic factors, industry factors and the broader corporate strategy. They can be analysed and optimized in conjunction with the major cross-functional partners and business leaders.

Conclusion

This chapter has discussed the importance of understanding workforce demand as it relates to the SWP process. To that end, it is crucial for the SWP practitioner to have a solid understanding of workforce demand and the factors that can affect this demand because this is essentially the starting point for building alignment with an organization's corporate strategy and its workforce strategy.

Understanding talent supply   04

CHAPTER OBJECTIVES

1 Learn the definition of talent supply and why it is important in SWP.

2 Learn how to assess the fundamental components of internal talent supply to include:

    a segmenting the workforce into critical and non-critical areas;

    b conducting a comprehensive skills/headcount inventory;

    c developing an attrition model/forecast;

    d identifying future skills requirements.

3 Learn how to assess the fundamental components of external talent supply to include:

    a new entrants into the labour market (usually through graduation from a university, college or trade school);

    b employees exiting the workforce due to retirement or change in career;

    c employees currently in the workforce in a chosen occupation.

Talent supply

In the previous chapter, a discussion was put forth on workforce demand along with a detailed breakdown of its components and an outline of how they factor into an organization's workforce strategy. This chapter will shift the focus from the demand for skills, experience and education to the supply of those same skills, experience and education.

Figure 4.1   Elements of workforce supply

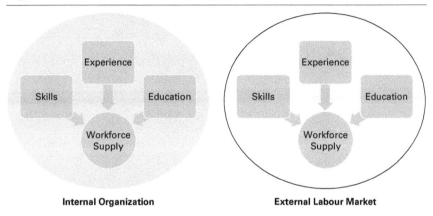

Internal Organization   **External Labour Market**

Workforce supply or talent supply is similar to workforce demand but differs in the sense that, rather than the literal need or demand for skills, experience and education by companies, industries and sectors (workforce demand), it is the actual availability of those skills, experience and education at any given time (Cascio and Aguinis, 2005). Think of workforce demand as what organizations 'need' from a talent perspective while thinking of talent supply as what is actually 'available' from a talent perspective. Like workforce demand, two key components make up talent supply. There is internal talent supply, which is the current and future composition of skills, experience and education that is or will be available to the organization, and there is external talent supply, which is the current and future availability in the labour market (see Figure 4.1).

Internal talent supply

Understanding an organization's talent supply is a critical aspect of any workforce strategy and can be thought of as an essential component of the SWP process. At the most fundamental level, the internal talent supply is the distribution of skills, experience and education that makes up the organization's workforce. It is important for organizations to understand their current and future supply of talent because it provides insight into where the company should be investing in talent. Understanding this will assist organizational leaders in being able to answer questions such as:

- What is the inventory of skills in key roles across the organization?

- On a scale of 1–10, how proficient are workers at these skills?

- Are there skills areas that we should invest more heavily in developing either today or in the future?

- Are the current skills in the organization still relevant?

- What skills will the organization require in the future? Are they different from the skills currently in place?

- Are the current headcount levels driving efficiency or redundancy?

- What is the experience level in the organization?

- Is the organization expanding into new product lines or markets that will require more experience?

- How do the skills, experience and education levels look across different locations and regions?

From these questions, it is apparent that the organization should have a firm grasp on its internal talent supply; however, how should it approach gaining insight into its current and future levels of talent? It is here that the role of SWP becomes critical. There are four primary activities that the SWP team will need to complete to have a comprehensive and holistic understanding of the organization's internal talent supply:

1 segmenting the workforce into critical and non-critical areas;

2 conducting a comprehensive skills/headcount inventory;

3 developing an attrition model/forecast;

4 identifying future skills requirements.

Workforce segmentation

The following entire chapter will discuss the topic of workforce segmentation (Chapter 5) so, for this section, the introduction to this concept will be brief. Workforce segmentation, as the name implies, segments the workforce into different categories. These categories can range from critical workforce segments to location-based workforce segments to skills-based workforce segments. Segmentation is based on the needs and priorities of the organization. Workforce segmentation is a critical component for understanding an organization's talent supply because it essentially applies the Pareto principle or the 80/20 rule to the organization's workforce (Reh, 2005). What this means is that there tends to be 20 per cent of the workforce that drives 80 per cent of the value.

Workforce segmentation is an important concept when developing a Strategic Workforce Plan because it provides a starting place for the organization to focus its efforts. When thinking about the company's talent supply, this concept becomes even more important. Why? Because a significant portion of the SWP talent supply process involves identifying skills and competency levels across the organization's workforce. Once skills deficiencies have been uncovered, identifying the critical workforce segments will provide a method of prioritization for the organization when deciding where to spend its training and development budgets.

Skills inventory

For an organization to maximize its productivity, it needs an efficient workforce. Becoming efficient or 'optimized' happens when HR and business leaders make good workforce-related policy decisions and when the workforce in question is fully skilled and competent at executing the day-to-day activities essential for productivity (Koch and McGrath, 1996). How does an organization gain insight into how qualified, skilled and experienced its workforce is? Answer: by conducting a skills inventory (Duffy, 2001).

Conducting a skills inventory is another SWP activity that requires a significant amount of cross-functional collaboration between the individuals involved in the SWP process, the HR department and the various business and team leaders. Because it can be a time-consuming exercise, it is good practice to begin the activity with either a critical workforce segment or as a smaller pilot project. The ultimate objective of conducting a skills inventory is to gauge, on a scale of 0–100 per cent (where 100 per cent is a workforce that is completely competent at a particular skill), how skilled the organization's workforce is at that skill. It is important to note, however, that each job or role in the organization will be likely to have several or even dozens of skills that will be required. It is easy to see, then, why this activity should be prioritized based on critical workforce segments and should involve cross-functional collaboration.

So, where to start? Before engaging in a full-blown enterprise-wide skills inventory project, it makes sense first to take on a pilot project, preferably with the aforementioned critical workforce segment. From there, the following steps can provide a reliable roadmap of actions to take:

1   Identify which skills or jobs will be in scope for the skills inventory project.

2   Identify a manager, leader or small team that is knowledgeable of the requisite skills for the jobs that are in scope for the project.

3   Develop two separate surveys:

   a   the first survey targets the manager who will rank each member of their team regarding their proficiency at the previously identified skill(s);

   b   the second survey will be one that focuses on the individual employees, rating their ability on the same skill set that the managers rated them on.

4   Multiply the total employees on the team involved in the analysis by the maximum proficiency score (which in this case is 10). For example, if 20 team members are required to have skill (X) then a fully proficient team would have a score of 200.

5   Have the team leader or manager conduct the skills ranking.

6   Aggregate the team leader's or manager's rankings across their entire team. For example, if there were 20 employees who all received a ranking of 7 for skill (X) the aggregate score would be 140.

7   Conduct the same activity in step six, but this time have the employees rank themselves.

8   Total the employee-level scores.

9   Average the employee-level scores and the manager-level scores.

10   Divide the averaged individual/manager scores by the maximum proficiency score to derive the skills proficiency level. For example, if the average manager/employee-level scores came out to 140 then the proficiency for the skill set in question would be 140/200 = 70 per cent.

11   Repeat this process for the top skills that make up a particular job or role.

Going through the exercise of conducting a skills inventory will be challenging, but equally rewarding regarding the level of insight managers will gain on the proficiency of critical skills and jobs in the organization. It will provide the SWP practitioner, HR leaders and managers with a baseline for understanding which skills require investment and help to drive a more optimally performing workforce.

Developing an attrition forecast

Attrition forecasting is another critical component of SWP. If an employee leaves (depending on the jobs, skills and strategy of the company), the company will have to replace that employee or risk losing the productivity they brought to the organization. Because of this, 'backfill' (filling positions that have become vacant due to attrition) is a significant component of the supply side of SWP.

A useful way to think about the impact that attrition can have on a company's workforce supply is to conduct the following activity. Forecast out the size of the company's workforce over a three or four-year period, then apply an attrition rate to the headcount for each of those years. Subtract the headcount lost due to attrition from the baseline number each year, and it quickly becomes apparent how the workforce dwindles in size from the impact of attrition. Completing this activity will also shed light on how hiring for backfill has the potential to make up a significant portion of an organization's sourcing efforts each year (see Figure 4.2).

Figure 4.2   The impact of attrition on an organization's talent supply before hiring for backfill

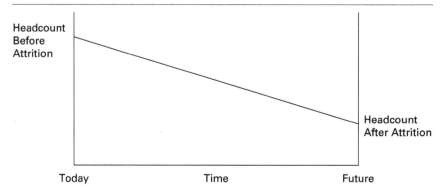

When building out attrition forecasts, it is important to recognize the different categories of attrition. Depending upon the use of the attrition forecast, the methodology required to create the forecast can vary dramatically. The first difference to consider is *regrettable versus non-regrettable attrition*. Regrettable attrition refers to the employees in an organization who, when gone, have the potential to impact productivity and other organizational performance factors negatively. Non-regrettable attrition, however, is the opposite. These are the employees who may not be performing well or are receiving high compensation relative to the value they are adding to the company's performance. In situations where attrition is non-regrettable, the organization is effectively saying it is happy to see these employees leave because they can find more productive employees elsewhere.

The next nuance in attrition definitions is the notion of *aggregate versus individual-level attrition*. Aggregate attrition refers to the total attrition for either the entire company or a particular segment within the company. In this example, if there have been an average of 100 employees in the organization over the past year and, over that same year, 10 per cent of them have left the organization, the aggregate attrition rate is 10 per cent. This means the organization might have been forced to hire 10 new employees to replace the ones that have left.

Individual-level attrition forecasting, on the other hand, refers to a type of attrition forecast that seeks to predict, on a more granular level, which employees are more likely to leave the organization *ceteris paribus* (all things being equal). The purpose of this type of attrition forecast is to develop a risk profile for employees who might be considering leaving the organization. Then, based on the profile of employees most likely to leave, develop retention strategies to help mitigate against the danger of these employees actually leaving. The biggest challenge with this form of attrition forecasting is that predicting attrition at this level of granularity sometimes can be perceived as a violation of privacy by the individual employees in question. To that end, it is important for the organization to be forthright and transparent when communicating to the workforce how and why the company is attempting to predict attrition at the individual level. In other words, it behoves the organization to create a communication strategy for the predictive forecast that puts a positive spin on how and why this type of forecast can and should be used to improve engagement, working conditions and culture such that employees will not want to leave the organization.

Attrition forecasting as it relates to SWP is important because it provides business and HR leaders with an understanding of how much of their workforce they can expect to lose in a given time period because of employees leaving. It is critical for these business and HR leaders to understand this because it will provide them with guidance on how many backfills they will need to hire for the time period in question. The paragraphs above discussed aggregate versus individual-level forecasting in the context of developing future workforce talent supply projections; as part of the Strategic Workforce Plan, aggregate-level forecasting is probably the most useful. To that end, several different forecasting techniques are helpful in predicting attrition at an aggregate level.

Naive forecast

A naive forecast is probably the most basic and least sophisticated form of attrition forecasting. In a naive forecast, the SWP practitioner takes the attrition rate from the previous period and applies it directly to the next period. This type of projection is useful when attrition levels are relatively stable with little variance. The biggest benefit here is the pure simplicity and interpretability of the model. The downside to this approach is the fact that the forecast is weighted 100 per cent on the lagging or past data observations.

Moving average

A moving average is another slightly more sophisticated form of a naive forecast. The moving average takes the average of a predefined set of periods from the past data and projects this average into the future. Moving averages can be useful when the data exhibit variability fluctuations. It is also a relatively simple calculation to perform and an easy model to build. The pitfall with this approach is that it tends to overly weight lagging or past data into the future. It is because of this fact that, like the naive forecast, the moving average is most useful when there is not a significant amount of change in attrition over time.

Time-series regression

A time series is a successive set of numbers collected over a set period of time (Hamilton, 1994). Time-series regression modelling is a form of statistical forecasting that models future events based on the past. It is most useful relative to the moving average and naive methods when events in the past are dynamic. In essence, it is the purest form of trend analysis. A time-series regression is almost identical to a linear regression except that, in the case of a time-series regression, the predictor variable is the time period itself, with the response variable in our case being a variable such as attrition.

Exponential smoothing

Exponential smoothing is a statistical technique that can be applied to time-series data with the objective of smoothing out some of the white noise that often exists in data sets of this nature (Gardner, 1985). In the moving average example, past observations are weighted equally but, when applying the smoothing technique, the most recent observations are weighted in an exponentially decreasing manner over time. This basically means that the most recent observations are considered more important than older observations in the time series. Exponential smoothing is a good method to use in conjunction with a time-series regression when it is not known if the variation in the data is random or white noise.

Auto-regressive integrated moving average (ARIMA)

An ARIMA model is one of the more advanced forms of forecasting attrition. An ARIMA model involves two components. The first is the AR or auto-regressive portion of the model. This part of the model regresses the lag of the variable of interest against itself. In the context of an ARIMA model, the moving average or MA portion of the model is different from how it was defined earlier. In an ARIMA model, the moving average part refers to the process of modelling the regression error terms as a linear combination of errors that occurred at various times in the past (Box *et al*, 2015). ARIMA modelling, although advanced, has the potential to be a valuable tool to have in the SWP practitioner's toolbox.

Author's note

The preceding discussion on statistical techniques provides very fundamental definitions of how these statistical methods work. More technical definitions of the maths of these statistical methodologies are outside the scope of this book, but exploring these techniques in more depth will be precious for any SWP practitioner wanting to provide a quantified approach to their SWP.

Future skills assessment

This will be discussed in greater detail later in the book, but the final aspect of the talent supply activity is equal parts brainstorming and looking into a crystal ball. The objective of this exercise is to work with business and HR leaders to identify what skills the organization might require in the future that are not in existence today. Although by no means a precise activity, the SWP practitioner should develop a series of questions to work through with these cross-functional partners, with the intention of bringing more focus to the brainstorming sessions. Some questions that might usefully stimulate the discussion include the following:

- What are the technological trends in the industry or sector in which our organization competes?
- Are technological advances going to complicate or simplify the way the organization conducts its work?
- If future technology is likely to require new skills, what might those skills be:
  - people-facing, sales or customer-service skills?
  - maths or science skills?
  - computer programming and engineering skills?
  - trades skills such as welders?
  - physical labour?
  - leadership skills?
  - cultural adaptability or language skills?
  - logistics skills (pilots, bus drivers or truck drivers)?

Figure 4.3 Evaluating the labour market for relevant skills

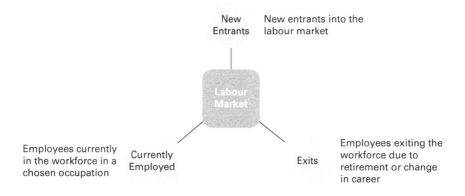

New Entrants — New entrants into the labour market

Labour Market

Employees currently in the workforce in a chosen occupation — Currently Employed

Exits — Employees exiting the workforce due to retirement or change in career

Once the list of potential future skills is complete, the strategic workforce practitioner should work with these same business and HR leaders to assign a series of probabilities to each skill based on the likelihood of the organization requiring these skills in the future. These probabilities should accompany a timeline for when the organization might require the skills. From this activity, the SWP practitioner can develop scenarios for the possibility of the organization legitimately requiring the skills along with starting to explore the external labour market for the availability of those skills.

External talent supply

Once the components of the internal talent supply are in place, the SWP practitioner needs to ensure they give an equal amount of attention to the external portion of the talent supply equation. External talent supply refers to the summation of skills, experience and education that exist in the labour market both today and in the future. Understanding trends regarding the external talent market is critical for a reliable workforce strategy. Why? Because if the organization merely assumes that the essential skills are available in the external market without verifying their existence, the organization could place its strategic objectives at risk if they are, in fact, not available. As illustrated in Figure 4.3, there are three components to consider when evaluating the labour market for a particular skill set or job:

- new entrants into the labour market (usually through graduation from a university, college or trade school);
- employees exiting the workforce due to retirement or change in career;
- employees currently in the workforce in a chosen occupation.

New entrants

Analysing the level of new entrants into the labour market is important because it can signify if any trends exist that might suggest there is an increase or decrease in interest for a particular degree or programme that could impact the supply of skills in the future. As an example, suppose admissions and graduates for finance degrees have decreased in number each year for the past five years. What might the impact of this trend have on the availability of finance professionals in the future? A real-world example of the impact and importance of understanding and analysing trends in the level of skills is the recent shortage of technical skills that has faced South Africa. The country's skills shortage has had a crippling effect on the economy and led to significant challenges for organizations in the country that rely on technical skills to execute on their business models (Rasool and Botha, 2011). Organizations that proactively tracked and analysed the labour market and the macroeconomic factors leading up to the skills shortage were better positioned to find the talent they required for their business operations than competitors who did not track and analyse that same talent market. Fortunately, from a data perspective, there are many rich data sources available that track trends of this nature such as the Bureau of Labor Statistics (BLS) in the United States and the Office for National Statistics in the United Kingdom. These data sources may vary from country to country, but generally speaking, some sort of statistics or government data are usually available for the analyst to explore as a starting point.

Employees exiting the workforce

Determining retirement and career changes can be much more challenging to ascertain than new entrants. Retirement rates by occupation do exist in some government statistics repositories, but can be inconsistent regarding their level of detail across professions.

Still, this is once again a good place to start from an exploratory data standpoint. Another approach could be to look at broader age demographics found in census data and apply some base line assumptions regarding the age of the population to data for individual occupations. In other words, if 5 per cent of the population is in a typical retirement age category, like 65, then it is reasonable to assume that 5 per cent of the population within the profession in question might be retiring as well. A quick word of caution with this approach, however: there are certain occupations where age distributions might skew in either direction on the age spectrum. For example, in a more contemporary professional occupation like a mobile software engineer (computer engineers who design apps for cellphones), there is likely to be a much smaller portion of the total workforce nearing retirement compared with a more traditional occupation like accounting. When making assumptions of this nature, the SWP professional should use their judgment and experience and partner with HR and business leaders to ensure those assumptions are accurate and representative of the population in question.

Employees currently in the workforce

Finally and most importantly, the SWP practitioner should factor in the current supply of skills, experience and education in the external labour market for the various organizational jobs in the scope for the workforce strategy and Strategic Workforce Plan. Two primary data sources are useful for this part of the analysis. The first is census and government data. Census data comprise a great source to establish a baseline for current levels of talent, but have similar limitations to retirement data (limited detail at the nuanced job level). Government job data also can vary by country, which has the potential to pose a challenge for organizations that are global in nature. Social media sites like LinkedIn can be another great source for assessing the labour market, especially when done in conjunction with government data. LinkedIn specifically is useful because it allows the analyst to evaluate talent supply levels by such factors as city, skill, education and experience level. To gain the maximum benefit from a social media site like LinkedIn, however, the organization will need to pay for a recruiter licence. There is value in paying for this service, however, because a licence of this nature will provide the analyst with more accurate statistics on the entire labour market. It would be impossible to get this level of accuracy with a basic LinkedIn profile, which is why you need a recruiter licence to take full advantage of the power of the platform.

The final method for assessing current talent levels is to utilize industry reports. Most industries publish summary reports that analyse labour supply and demand dynamics. Often, the organization will have to pay for these reports, but there are some that are free and easy to find with a quick Google search. As with the other data sources in this section, industry reports can vary dramatically, depending on the industry and region, so there is no guarantee that they will exist. That said, it is worth doing some research because, if they do exist, these industry reports can be a very rich source of data to supplement additional data sources.

Summary of chapter objectives

Why talent supply is important in SWP

Workforce supply is an essential component of any thoughtful Strategic Workforce Plan. It refers to both the internal and external supply of talent. Talent supply in this context is the summation of skills, experience and education. Talent supply is related to talent demand, with the main difference being that talent supply is what talent actually exists, either today or in the future, while talent demand refers to what the organization would like to have either today or in the future. Like workforce demand, talent supply has two critical components that the organization should consider when developing a Strategic Workforce Plan. Those two elements are internal talent and external talent supply.

How to assess the fundamental components of internal talent supply

Internal talent supply consists of the total skills, experience and education that exist within an organization today and also what that supply of skills, experience and education will look like in the future. To understand what the internal talent supply looks like within an organization, it is essential for the SWP practitioner to partner with HR business partners and business leaders in a series of activities that seek to shed light on what the true supply of talent looks like currently and will look like in the future. Those key activities include:

- segmenting the workforce into critical and non-critical areas;
- conducting a comprehensive skills/headcount inventory;
- developing an attrition model/forecast;
- identifying future skills requirements.

A detailed breakdown of specific actions required for these activities can be found earlier in this chapter.

How to assess the fundamental components of external talent

External talent supply, on the other hand, refers to the summation of skills, experience and education that exist in the external labour market. It is important to understand external talent supply in the context of what exists today and what will exist in the future. Understanding this dynamic is important because, when developing a Strategic Workforce Plan, the availability of certain skill sets is a key component involved in ensuring the organization will have access to the talent it requires to execute on its organizational strategy. If, however, the SWP practitioner does not factor in the future landscape of talent in their Strategic Workforce Plan, the organization might be at risk of not being able to access the aforementioned skills. There are three key aspects of assessing the external talent market that the SWP practitioner should seek to understand while developing an assessment of the external talent market:

- new entrants into the labour market (usually through graduation from a university, college or trade school);
- employees exiting the workforce due to retirement or change in careers;
- employees currently in the workforce in a chosen occupation.

From a data perspective, assessing these three components can be challenging. But fortunately, with some creativity and research, discovering insights from a variety of data sources is entirely possible. Three of these data sources are:

- government data in the form of census and job codes and trends;
- social media sites like LinkedIn and Entelo;
- industry reports on relevant labour statistics.

Understanding the supply of talent is a foundational aspect of the SWP process. It helps business and HR leaders to understand what the current state of talent looks like from both the internal and external perspectives, as well as helping those leaders gain insight into what that talent will look like in the future. The criticality of understanding the supply of talent and, more specifically, the distribution and level of skills that organizations possess is a crucial component of SWP that will continue to be highlighted as an area of importance throughout this book.

Workforce segmentation 05

CHAPTER OBJECTIVES

1 Outline the concept of workforce segmentation and why it is important in SWP.

2 Outline the factors that distinguish a critical workforce segment from a regular workforce segment:

a availability of skills in the external market;

b the segment has a disproportionate impact on the organization's value chain;

c the segment has a disproportionate impact on business outcomes.

3 Describe other variations of workforce segmentation.

4 Describe the prioritization of workforce segmentation for a Strategic Workforce Plan.

Workforce segmentation

When it comes to SWP, the concept of workforce segmentation is critical. As nice as it would be to have all the roles and skills in the organization driving equal impact and value for the organization's bottom line, the reality is that, in the world of SWP, all roles and skills are not equal. So, why is this and what does it have to do with workforce segmentation and SWP? The most fundamental concept behind workforce segmentation centres on the notion that, when it comes to investing in and developing the workforce, there should be some practical measures in place to ensure that the organization is prioritizing the roles that are driving value in the organization. Lavelle (2007) states that 'workforce segmentation seeks not to differentiate performance or individual contributions but rather distinguish between roles and skill sets in terms of how vital they are to business success'. Naturally, to create an optimized Strategic Workforce Plan, it is the SWP practitioner who will be likely to be the first stakeholder seeking to understand which segments are driving value and how they should prioritize those segments for the plan.

Vilfredo Pareto was an Italian economist in the 19th century who developed the economic theory called the Pareto principle to help describe wealth distribution in Italy during his era. The rule states that, in a normal distribution, 80 per cent of the output comes from 20 per cent of the input. In the context of SWP, the Pareto principle, or the 80/20 rule, is a useful method for thinking about productivity because it can be used to describe individual or aggregate-level productivity. At the individual employee level, it is likely that 80 per cent of the value that employees add comes from only 20 per cent of the tasks they complete. Similarly, at the organization level, it is likely that 80 per cent of the value created on a monthly, quarterly or yearly basis comes from within 20 per cent of the organization (Reh, 2005). It is easy to see how the Pareto principle can be a powerful tool for the SWP practitioner to include in their toolkit. Applying the Pareto principle to the workforce (see Figure 5.1) transforms the notion of workforce segments, which one might misinterpret as being equal,

Figure 5.1   Applying the Pareto principle to workforce segmentation

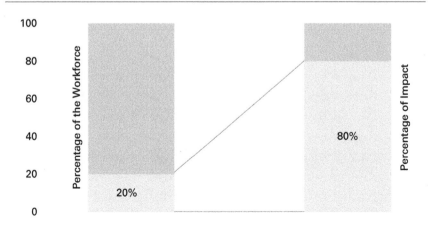

to the concept of 'critical workforce segments', which, as described earlier, implies they are not equal. Adding the term '*critical*' to the phrase 'workforce segments' removes any ambiguity around the fact that priority levels for these workforce segments are not the same and as such they should not receive equal treatment when it comes to prioritizing, planning and investing.

Identifying workforce segments

To take full advantage of the usefulness of workforce segmentation, the SWP practitioner must first be able to determine what constitutes a workforce segment. Like many topics in this book, the criteria that define a workforce segment in one organization may differ dramatically in another organization. Depending on the industry, business or location, workforce segments can take on various forms. To that end, it is essential for the SWP practitioner to remember that the primary benefit of workforce segmentation as it relates to the Strategic Workforce Plan is to provide a method for prioritizing risk mitigation and investment across the company's workforce. The secondary benefit of workforce segmentation is the ability to analyse the workforce via different segments or 'cuts of the data'.

Features of workforce segmentation

Regarding the main advantage of workforce segmentation, while it is possible to segment the workforce by categories such as location, it should be kept in mind that, ultimately, the goal should be to divide the labour force into segments that drive a disproportionate amount of value. So, where should the SWP practitioner start when it comes to identifying segments that are critical to the organization's success? As shown in Figure 5.2, there tend to be three features that critical workforce segments possess that can provide a starting place to help the SWP practitioner assess and identify these segments:

- a segment of the workforce where the skills make-up of that segment tends to be in high demand or low supply relative to the skills in other segments of the organization;

Figure 5.2   Key features of a critical workforce segment

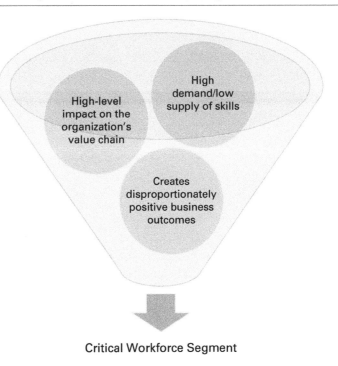

High-level
impact on the
organization's
value chain

High
demand/low
supply of skills

Creates
disproportionately
positive business
outcomes

Critical Workforce Segment

- a segment of the workforce that has a disproportionate impact on the organization's value chain;
- a segment of the workforce that drives a disproportionate number of positive business outcomes.

Workforce segmentation steps

The first place to start when attempting to identify critical workforce segments is with the skill sets that are in high demand and short supply in the external labour market. The reason this can be a good indicator is that, when a set of skills or a job type is valuable to one company, it is likely that the same skill set or job type also will be valuable to the company's competitors. Roles for which recruiting and retaining employees is more difficult are likely to equate to those roles being critical. A good example of this is in the oil and gas industry, where petroleum engineers are typically in high demand and short supply (more so when oil prices are high, and the industry is booming). It is not coincidental, then, that petroleum engineers are high on the list of critical roles for most if not all organizations operating in this industry.

So how, specifically, can the SWP practitioner use this approach to develop a list of roles that could fall into a critical category or segment? They should start by reaching out to the talent acquisition team and asking this team the question: what roles are more difficult to recruit for and why? From there they should move to the data and look at metrics such as average time to fill and attrition rates. Are there certain roles that have a significantly longer recruiting life cycle than others? What about attrition? Is there a correspondingly high attrition rate for these same roles? Could this be because there is such high demand in the external market for these roles that employees with these skill sets working in these roles have more opportunities than those in less high demand roles? From talking with the recruiters and analysing these data points, the SWP practitioner should have a good place to start regarding the identification of roles that fall into critical workforce segments.

The next place to utilize when identifying critical workforce segments is through the organization's value chain. To do this, however, first requires an understanding of what a value chain is. So, to that end, what is an organizational value chain? First described by Michael Porter in his book *Competitive Advantage: Creating and Sustaining Superior Performance* (2008), we learn that a value chain is a series of the main activities and supporting activities that, when combined, form a system of processes and sub-processes having the potential to add or detract value from the organization's core product or service offering. In Porter's original book, the value chain was used to describe the manufacturing of a product from end to end, which involved the following key activities:

- inbound logistics;
- operations;
- outbound logistics;
- marketing and sales;
- service.

And a series of supporting activities:

- firm infrastructure;
- HR management;
- technology;
- procurement.

The underlying concept of Porter's model is that an organization can improve the inputs and outputs via optimizing processes and decisions along each link in the value chain. The final output in this paradigm is an increase in the company's operating margins or profit. While this model clearly skews towards product development in a manufacturing setting, the core activities can be changed depending upon the industry or sector in which an organization operates.

So, what does the value chain have to do with identifying critical workforce segments? It provides the SWP practitioner with another reliable methodology or starting point for prioritizing which roles should be considered essential and which ones should not. For example, once the SWP practitioner has identified the core activities that make up their value chain, they can further break down that particular area of the value chain into roles that fall under these core activities. Let us use sales and marketing as an example of an activity to analyse for possible critical workforce segments. In this example, the question that the SWP practitioner should be asking is: what are the roles that are contributing the most to adding value (increasing profit) to the sales and marketing activity? The answer is likely to be that, within sales and marketing, the sales roles that are going out and selling or creating new revenue are likely to be the roles most critical to adding value to this activity. Continuing this process across all of the primary and secondary activities for the organization's value chain will shed additional light on which segments are critical or not critical.

The final step for identifying critical workforce segments involves assessing the organization against impactful or positive business outcomes. Of the three methods, this is the most subjective and requires the closest partnership with business leaders to define what constitutes an impactful or positive business outcome. It is important to note that there is a high probability of there being a close relationship between how the organization defines impactful business outcomes and the key areas described in the value chain section. In other words, it should not be a surprise if marketing and sales meet the criteria for being a critical activity in the organization's value chain and, at the same time, produce some of the largest business impacts and outcomes. Where the two approaches diverge is that the value chain is focused solely on activities that either decrease or increase the operating margins, while the definition of impactful business outcomes can encompass a much broader array of activities.

So, what sort of business impact, and roles related to that impact, should the SWP practitioner be attempting to identify? A good tactic for approaching this assessment is to ask the following question: if everyone in the organization decided to take a week off from work at the same time, what are the roles that would have the largest negative impact on the organization? More specifically, what are the roles in this scenario that, if not in place, would disrupt the organization from being able to operate smoothly and accomplish its short-term, day-to-day activities? In this part of the assessment, it is likely that roles such as project managers, systems engineers, recruiters and even custodial positions will come to the forefront as being critical. If, from this evaluation, roles are identified that may not seem critical, it should be acknowledged that this is okay and, in fact, should be expected. The whole purpose of going through this activity is to ensure all the key roles have been identified, not just the roles that are intuitively critical.

Additional forms of workforce segmentation

Segmenting the workforce based on critical roles is not the only approach that organizations can take with regards to broader workforce segmentation. Organizations can segment the workforce based on a multitude of different factors to include segmentation based on internal or external business drivers, different functions in the organization, experience level, leadership and contingent versus FTE workers.

Segmentation based on business drivers

In this form of segmentation, the SWP practitioner is looking to align and prioritize the segmentation of roles based on factors that are driving the business either internally or externally or both. Segmentation based on business drivers may sound similar to business outcome/impact segmentation, but there are differences and nuances between the two. The main difference between this approach and the other is that, in this method, rather than applying the Pareto principle to specific roles, the SWP practitioner includes all the roles that contribute to business impact through specific internal or external factors. For example, if the number of aircraft engines manufactured is a key business driver, the SWP practitioner might ask the question: what are all the roles – end to end – involved in the manufacturing of an aircraft engine? In the business outcome/impact example, the SWP practitioner probably would have said that the majority of segmentation focus should be on engineers. In this case, however, they are saying that all of the roles involved in the manufacturing of an engine should make up a workforce segment. The prioritization portion of this form of workforce segmentation comes through in comparing all the different business driver segments to assess which ones are more critical to the organization's mission.

Continuing with this example, the SWP practitioner could examine the business driver segment most closely associated with manufacturing engines against a separate business driver such as the number of new products/engines developed. They could assess these two segments through the lens of the organization's long-term vision. Maybe the answer ends up being that the organization's success depends more on the number of new engines/products being developed than those currently being manufactured, which would lead to prioritizing the new products/engines segment over the manufacturing of engines segment.

Segmenting the workforce based on location

Segmentation through location is another potential approach to segmenting the workforce. When segmenting the workforce by location, the SWP practitioner is taking a step back to analyse the workforce for the entire organization, but doing it specifically at the site level. Like the other segmentation activities, the objective that the SWP process is striving for with this approach is to categorize the workforce based on business impact or added value but, in this case, doing it at each location where the company operates. To assess and segment the workforce at the site level, the SWP practitioner should be asking a series of questions regarding the structure of the workforce and the day-to-day activities that take place at each location. The SWP practitioner should ask these questions in the context of the broader organizational mission and strategy, possibly including questions such as:

- Does this location own or support a particular activity?
- Are locations dispersed globally?
- Is the location a cost centre or a profit centre or both?
  - If both, how much of the location is profit versus cost centre?
- How productive is the location?
- What is the cost of labour in the location's local market?
- What is the cost of living for the location?
- Do the locations operate autonomously or through guidance from headquarters?
- What is the make-up of skills in this location?
  - Are they technical, trades or professional?
- What is the availability of skills in the location's local market?
  - Are those skills aligned with daily work requirements for the location?
- What is the tenure make-up for the location?

Before answering these questions, the SWP practitioner and organizational leaders should agree on the criteria that will be used to prioritize and rank the locations for segmentation. Depending upon the organization's priorities and where the organization is in its life cycle, the type of criteria for this can vary. The following list of possible criteria provides a starting point for the SWP practitioner to consider when prioritizing location segments:

- weight locations higher that are primarily profit centres;
- weight locations higher that have more technical or difficult skills to source;
- weight locations with greater productivity higher;
- weight locations higher that focus on manufacturing or delivering services that heavily factor into the organization's future strategy.

Broad-category segmentation

In addition to the more complete forms of segmentation discussed in this chapter thus far, segmenting the workforce into more general categories can be useful as well. In this type of workforce segmentation, the SWP practitioner is looking to classify workforce segments into groups of two or three. While this approach to workforce segmentation can still be helpful for prioritizing workforce-related investments, it tends to be more impactful as a method for breaking the workforce down into categories that are easier to analyse. Workforce segmentation of this nature can be a valuable tool for organizations that are smaller in size, where splitting the workforce into 10 or 15 different categories might not be practical or even provide the SWP practitioner with enough data points to derive any useful insights from the data. Examples of broad workforce segmentation include segmenting the workforce by the following:

- contractor versus contingent worker versus FTE;
- hourly versus salary;
- junior versus senior;
- manager versus individual contributor;
- tenure bands;
- business units;
- functions;
- performance ratings;
- generational age groups.

Segmenting the workforce based on critical roles is not the only approach that organizations can take with regards to broader workforce segmentation. Organizations can segment the workforce based on a multitude of different factors to include segmentation based on internal or external business drivers, functions, experience level, leadership and contingent versus FTE workers. The SWP practitioner should have a relatively clear idea in mind regarding how they will use the workforce segmentation data before coming to a final decision regarding the approach to segmenting the workforce. Defining the use-case for workforce segmentation data is important, because without it the organization risks wasting valuable time and resources on activities that do not lead to actionable results. For example, without a clear vision of how the organization will use the data outputs from a workforce segmentation activity, the SWP practitioner might be tempted to segment the workforce by all the dimensions mentioned above. The question is, will these different cuts of the data be useful and, moreover, are they even required? To that end, the question of how the organization will use the segmented data to make decisions definitely should be asked.

Prioritizing workforce segments

After the SWP practitioner has worked with organizational leaders to come up with a strategy for segmenting the workforce, the time will come to go through the activity of prioritizing those segments. Although not as time-consuming as going through the actual segmentation process, developing a point of view regarding prioritization of the segments is equally important. Why? Because how the segments land on the prioritization matrix will have a large impact on where the organization makes resourcing and other strategic decisions for the organization's workforce.

Prioritization of the workforce segments is dependent upon how the organization plans to use those workforce segments in the broader Strategic Workforce Plan. If the segments are treated equally in the plan, it is likely that the activity of workforce segmentation was only designed to provide categories to make analysing the workforce easier. In this case, prioritization of the segments will not be necessary. On the other hand, if the intent of the workforce segmentation exercise was to help the organization make better decisions regarding workforce investment and retention strategies, prioritizing these segments will be necessary.

The prioritization process begins by having a discussion with organizational and HR leaders concerning the topic of how these segments will factor into the final Strategic Workforce Plan. The aim of this review should be to come to a final decision regarding the types of decisions the organization can make using the workforce segmentation data. From these discussions, the SWP practitioner along with organizational and HR leaders should be able to answer the following questions:

- If we had US $1000 to spend on improving the efficiency of the workforce, where should we spend it?
- If we had US $1000 to spend on retention strategies for the workforce, where should we spend it?
- If we had US $1000 to spend on attracting top talent to the organization, where should we spend it?
- If we could allocate US $1000 across the three strategies mentioned above, how would that allocation look?

Before answering these questions, the SWP practitioner should once again work with organizational and HR leaders to ensure that the critical workforce-related challenges have been identified. In these conversations, the group should be thinking about topics like:

- Is attrition an issue in the organization?
- How much of an impact on the organization's bottom line would incremental improvements in productivity have?
- Is attracting top talent a challenge?
- Will attracting top talent become more important moving into the future?

Answering these questions should lead to two distinct outcomes. The first is a better understanding, agreement and point of view on whether there will be one or multiple prioritization decisions made from the workforce segmentation data. The second, based on the identification of workforce segments, is a list that ranks and prioritizes these segments. Once this is complete, the SWP practitioner can begin the process of incorporating these segments into the final Strategic Workforce Plan. On this topic, it is worth noting that workforce segments and the priority of these workforce segments can and probably will change over time. The prioritization of workforce segments is yet another reason why it is important to acknowledge that a good Strategic Workforce Plan is a dynamic and evolving process/plan. It should be regularly revisited for this very reason and should be something that changes as often as the environment in which the organization operates changes.

Summary of chapter objectives

The concept of workforce segmentation and why it is important in SWP

Workforce segmentation is an approach to SWP whereby the SWP practitioner creates different categories for the workforce based on the specific needs of the organization. Workforce segmentation can be especially useful to the company when the workforce segments are prioritized based on the criticality of the roles in those segments. Positions identified as being 'critical' make up critical workforce segments. Typically, critical workforce segments are made up of 20 per cent of the positions in an organization that create 80 per cent of the value. Being able to differentiate critical workforce segments from non-critical workforce segments can be a valuable method for making decisions concerning where to invest in the workforce.

Distinguishing a critical workforce segment from a regular workforce segment

In this chapter we learned that, although various factors contribute to labelling a workforce segment as critical, three factors specifically stand out as being key contributors to critical workforce segments:

- a segment of the workforce where the skills make-up of that segment tends to be in high demand or low supply relative to the skills in other segments of the organization;
- a segment of the workforce that has a disproportionate impact on the organization's value chain;
- a segment of the workforce that drives a disproportionate number of positive business outcomes.

Other variations of workforce segmentation

This chapter also outlined the following three additional variations of workforce segmentation.

Segmentation based on business drivers

In this form of segmentation, the SWP practitioner is looking to align and prioritize the segmentation of roles based on factors that are driving the business either internally or externally or both.

Segmentation based on location

Segmentation through location is another potential approach to segmenting the workforce. When segmenting the workforce by location, the SWP practitioner is taking a step back to analyse the workforce for the entire organization, but doing it specifically at the site level. Like the other segmentation activities, the objective the SWP practitioner is striving for with this approach is to categorize the workforce based on business impact or added value but, in this case, doing it at each location where the company operates.

Broad-category segmentation

In this type of workforce segmentation, the SWP practitioner is looking to classify workforce segments into groups of two or three. While this approach to workforce segmentation can still be helpful for prioritizing workforce-related investments, it tends to be more impactful as a method for breaking the workforce down into categories that are easier to analyse. Workforce segmentation of this nature can be a valuable tool for organizations that are smaller in size, where splitting the workforce into 10 or 15 different categories might not be practical or even provide the SWP practitioner with enough data points to derive any useful insights from the data. Examples of broad workforce segmentation include segmenting the workforce by:

- contractor versus contingent worker versus FTE;
- hourly versus salary;
- junior versus senior;
- manager versus individual contributor;
- tenure bands;
- business units;
- functions;
- performance ratings;
- generational age groups.

Prioritizing workforce segments

Once the SWP practitioner has segmented the workforce, they will need to work with organizational and HR leaders to determine how the organization will prioritize those workforce segments for the Strategic Workforce Plan. The prioritization process begins by having a discussion with corporate and HR leaders around the topic of how these segments will factor into the final Strategic Workforce Plan. The aim of this review should be to come to a final decision regarding the types of decisions the organization makes regarding the workforce segmentation data. From these discussions, the SWP practitioner, organizational and HR leaders should be able to answer the following questions:

- If we had US $1000 to spend on improving the efficiency of the workforce, where should we spend it?
- If we had US $1000 to spend on retention strategies for the workforce, where should we spend it?
- If we had US $1000 to spend on attracting top talent to the organization, where should we spend it?
- If we could allocate US $1000 across the three strategies mentioned above, how would that allocation look?

Before answering these questions, the SWP practitioner should once again work with organizational and HR leaders to ensure that the critical workforce-related challenges have been identified. In these conversations, the group should be thinking through questions such as:

- Is attrition an issue in the organization?
- How much of an impact on the organization's bottom line would incremental improvements in productivity have?
- Is attracting top talent a challenge?
- Will attracting top talent become more important moving into the future?

Conclusion

This chapter has provided the reader with an overview of the definition of workforce segmentation and critical workforce segments, a framework for how to identify workforce segments and, finally, a methodology for prioritizing and using these segments to gain the most value in the SWP process. The book will continue to build on the workforce segmentation framework, and the tools learned in this chapter, if applied correctly, can provide more ammunition for the organization as it builds out its SWP arsenal, continuing to add value to the organization.

Total cost of the workforce

CHAPTER OBJECTIVES

1 Define cost-based SWP.

2 Outline the categories of workforce costs:

  a fixed costs;

  b variable costs;

  c tangible costs;

  d intangible costs;

  e opportunity costs.

3 Define HR programme costs.

4 Describe how to include costs in the Strategic Workforce Plan.

Cost-based SWP

This chapter will discuss the role of workforce costs in the SWP process. To provide deeper context around the importance of accounting for workforce-related costs in a Strategic Workforce Plan, let us explore the fundamental reason why most business owners start companies in the first place, which arguably is to earn profits and increase shareholder value (Rappaport, 1986). The statement that the primary purpose of a business is to make money is an over-simplified and capitalistic approach to describing why businesses are started, but it is useful in trying to emphasize the importance of accounting for costs in the SWP process, which will be discussed in more detail below.

If the primary purpose of a business is to create wealth for the business owners (shareholders), it stands to reason that most organizations create their corporate strategies based on the intention of adding value (creating wealth) for these owners. If this is the driving factor for developing a business strategy, how do companies create these strategies? There are dozens of strategic methods for increasing shareholder value but, fundamentally and from a balance sheet perspective, there are four primary tactics that the enterprise can focus on to increase value:

- increasing revenue;
- managing the organization's assets efficiently;
- managing investor expectations;
- controlling operating margins.

The first tactic for increasing shareholder value is to ensure that the organization has systems and an operating model in place that provides steady growth for the organization's revenue. The importance of consistent revenue growth for increasing shareholder value is the reason why the term 'chasing next corner's earnings' is often thrown around in business articles and television reports.

The next method for increasing shareholder value is to manage the organization's assets efficiently. This means the organization should ensure the assets the company invests in will generate more revenue to create more assets. In theory, this continual process will increase the value of the company (see above) and is the reason the stock market places great emphasis on managing assets efficiently.

Another factor that affects shareholder value is the expectations that investors have regarding the performance of the organization. When external investor sentiment is positive regarding the company's future, the company will be likely to attract more investors. With more investors investing in the company (assuming the company is publicly traded), the stock price or value of the enterprise continues to grow. On the flip side, if investor sentiment is negative, the company will be likely to lose investors, which will lead to a decrease in stock price or shareholder value. One of the most effective methods for the business to ensure it meets investor expectations is to clearly articulate how it will increase revenue, manage costs and utilize its assets efficiently. If the company can do this successfully, the current investors will be happy, and potential investors will invest in the company, thereby driving up the value of the business for its shareholders.

The final factor that affects shareholder value deals with managing the organization's operating margins. Here, the company is effectively trying to control its costs. As it relates to workforce costs and SWP, this is the most relevant factor for the SWP practitioner to consider. Why is this factor more relevant than the others for SWP? Because it deals most closely with organizational costs. Furthermore, it encompasses selling, general and administrative (SG&A) expenses which account for the majority of 'people-related' costs in most organizations. SG&A expenses are an important starting point for the SWP practitioner to think through if they are going to factor the total cost of the workforce into the Strategic Workforce Plan.

Bringing it back full circle, if the primary purpose of a business is to increase shareholder value, and if controlling workforce-related costs is one of the methods that organizations can use to ensure the creation of shareholder value, it is not surprising that the SWP practitioner should factor costs into their final Strategic Workforce Plan.

There is usually a relatively clear relationship between a company's ability to manage its costs and its profitability and performance (Kaplan and Cooper, 1998). That said, how should the SWP practitioner think about expenses and costs in the context of the broader Strategic Workforce Plan? The SWP practitioner should think of costs associated with workforce or HR programmes as constraints that the organization needs to factor in to reach an 'optimal' workforce state. What this means is that, when the final Strategic Workforce Plan is in place, there should be costs associated with all the forecasts and scenarios that account for factors such as headcount growth or retraction, location planning, training and development payroll and other workforce-related programmes (Cascio, 1986). Assigning costs to all of these factors will give the SWP practitioner a baseline for assessing a metric known as the *total cost of the workforce* (TCOW; see Figure 6.1). Intuitively, a Strategic Workforce Plan that tries to minimize the TCOW while at the same time increasing efficiency and

Figure 6.1 Developing a TCOW metric

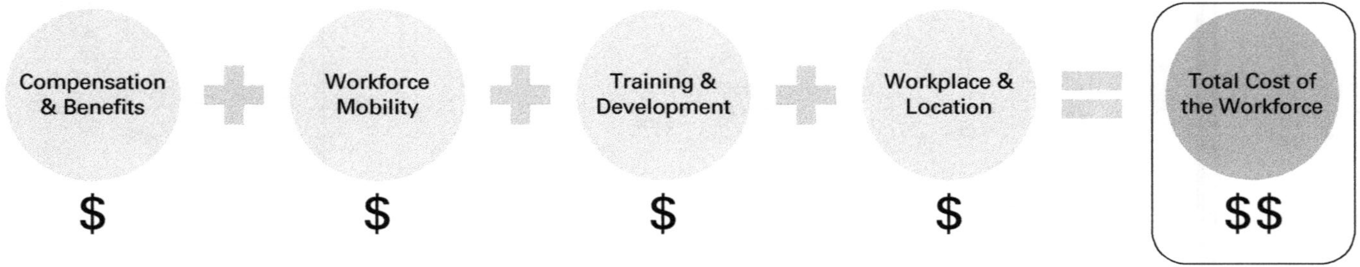

Compensation & Benefits
$

+

Workforce Mobility
$

+

Training & Development
$

+

Workplace & Location
$

=

Total Cost of the Workforce
$$

productivity in the workforce will be a Strategic Workforce Plan that is well positioned for helping the organization to perform well. One of the benefits of establishing the TCOW is that, when this metric is in place, the company can measure the performance of its workforce strategy by the costs associated with managing and growing the workforce. When workforce-related costs are growing higher than productivity and efficiency gains, it is a sign that the workforce strategy the organization is pursuing is not optimal. On the flip side, when costs are shrinking relative to the productivity, performance and efficiency of its workforce, the organization is executing well on its Strategic Workforce Plan. One of the main advantages of including costs in a Strategic Workforce Plan is that it gives the SWP practitioner the ability to work with business and HR leaders to create scenarios that model out different cost-benefit structures for workforce-related decisions. Including costs as a constraint in various what-if scenarios can help SWP practitioners to answer questions such as:

- What will be the impact on productivity if training and development spend is shifted by 10 per cent from Workforce Segment A to Workforce Segment B?

- What would be the impact from a cost perspective and an attracting and retaining talent perspective if the company doubled the number of days allocated for parental leave?

- What would be the impact on costs and productivity if the company reduced headcount growth targets by 5 per cent over the following two years?

- What would be the impact on costs and productivity if the company increased headcount growth targets by 5 per cent over the following two years?

- What would be the impact on costs and leadership development if the company discontinued its international rotational programme for developing leaders?

- What would be the impact on costs, employee engagement and productivity if the company decided to offer free meals to employees?

Through these questions, and others not included in the list here, it becomes quite apparent that, when making workforce-related decisions, both the cost and the perceived value or benefit of the new policy or programme should be analysed side-by-side. Doing this will provide the organization and the SWP practitioner with insight into whether the workforce-related decisions the organization is making are optimal.

Types of workforce costs

If the SWP practitioner is to take full advantage of the benefits of including workforce costs in their Strategic Workforce Plan, they must first understand the various types of workforce costs that could potentially be included in the plan. There are a wide array of costs and expenses the organization incurs that could be in scope for inclusion in the workforce plan. As shown in Figure 6.2, these costs typically fall into five broad categories: fixed costs, variable costs, tangible costs, intangible costs and opportunity costs. It is important to note that often there is crossover between these costs. Tangible costs have the potential to be either fixed or variable in nature. That

Figure 6.2 Different types of costs to consider in SWP

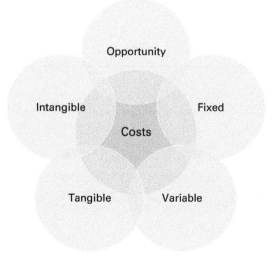

said, the following descriptions are intended to provide the reader with an overview of what these costs are, independent of their interaction across the categories.

Fixed costs

A fixed cost is a cost that reoccurs at some fixed interval and generally does not vary much regarding the amount of cost the company incurs (McEachern, 2011). An example of a fixed cost is the cost associated with the salary a company pays to its salaried employees. A company is required to pay its salaried employees a fixed amount once or twice a month. An important aspect to understand regarding fixed costs is the fact that the company incurs these costs independent of any business impact or results that are realized because of the cost. In other words, the organization has to pay these employees a set amount regardless of their performance or how much they contributed to the organization's success during the period in question. It is crucial to highlight that this example only applies to employees who receive a salary. Employees that receive commissions or hourly wages fall under a separate category which we will discuss in the following section.

Variable costs

Variable costs are another form of cost that the SWP practitioner should consider when thinking through the types of workforce-related costs to account for in the final Strategic Workforce Plan. A variable cost, as opposed to a fixed cost, is one that changes depending on some circumstance in the business (McEachern, 2011). In the salaried employee example above, the employee receives a fixed amount of cash each pay period regardless of what or how much they produce. For non-exempt (hourly) employees and commission-based employees, the same rule is not valid. In the case of these employees, the amount of cash they receive is dependent upon the amount of time they work and the level of sales they achieve. A key point for the SWP practitioner to consider regarding variable costs is that these costs are directly related to a business outcome. In other words, if the sales person in the organization makes a deal that requires a commission payout, the amount of that sale will have a direct impact on the organization's revenue. In the case of an hourly worker, if that employee works eight hours a day on a factory floor manufacturing widgets, and in those eight hours manufactures eight widgets a day, if that employee were to work nine hours in a day, they would produce one additional widget or nine widgets for the day. What this means is that their productivity output is a function of the number of hours they work in a given day. From these examples, it is evident, then, how costs have the potential to vary depending upon the productivity and operating conditions present in the employees' work environment.

Tangible costs

The SWP practitioner should also become familiar with the next class of costs which includes the concept of tangible versus intangible costs. Any expenses or costs that are real and that the company pays can be classified as tangible costs. Moreover, these are costs that the company has to account for and report in its financial statements. Both fixed and variable costs are examples of tangible costs because they are 'real' costs that the firm actually incurs. Payroll, HRIS software, consulting support and learning and development software and licences are all examples of tangible costs related to the organization's people, HR and the SG&A budget.

Intangible costs

Understanding the concept of tangible costs is relatively straightforward. Where things get a little less clear, however, is with the introduction of the notion of intangible and opportunity costs. Unlike tangible costs, which are real and easily accounted for in the organization's financial statements, intangible costs are not as easy to explain. Intangible costs are costs that occur 'behind the scenes', but cannot necessarily be quantified. These costs typically are related to productivity and another form of cost known as an opportunity cost. An example of an intangible cost is the cost associated with having a workforce with low employee engagement. If a hypothetical organization has a workforce lacking in engagement, it is likely that this low engagement, in turn, will lead to low productivity. The loss of productivity due to low engagement in the workforce is an example of an intangible cost. For obvious reasons, it is difficult to quantify from a financial perspective exactly how much the loss of productivity will cost the organization. Although it is hard to quantify, however, there should be little debate that the company is still incurring a cost it should account for or at least acknowledge in the Strategic Workforce Plan.

So, what are some examples of intangible workforce costs? The following list provides a starting point for the SWP practitioner to consider when going through the activity of identifying intangible or opportunity costs:

- cost of attrition (knowledge drain);
- cost of training a new employee (lost productivity while the employee learns their new job);
- cost of low employee engagement (less engaged employees are usually less productive);
- cost of leave of absence (lost productivity due to not being in the office);
- cost of poor organizational design (loss of productivity due to duplicate efforts or misaligned tasks).

Opportunity costs

An opportunity cost is a form of intangible cost. An opportunity cost is one the organization incurs for missing an opportunity because of a decision to pursue an alternative opportunity instead. For example, assume that a company has the budget to invest in a training programme. Now, consider that this company has the *opportunity* to invest in training programme A or training programme B. If the company decides to invest in training programme A, the company will sacrifice all of the benefits and productivity gains that might have been possible had the decision been made to invest in training programme B. The costs associated with foregoing these gains are considered to be opportunity costs.

Accounting for both tangible and intangible costs in the Strategic Workforce Plan (and, to a lesser degree, opportunity costs) is important because, if the SWP practitioner only considers tangible costs in their plan, they will have failed to determine the true cost of the workforce. The fallout for not identifying the true TCOW in the final Strategic Workforce Plan is that the organization could potentially be making ill-informed or inadequate workforce and HR programme-related decisions. Intuitively, this could lead to sub-optimal organizational performance in the future.

HR programme costs

Once the SWP practitioner has a solid understanding of the different types of costs, it is important to shift focus to thinking more about the specific costs, usually tangible, that the organization's HR programmes incur. It is critical for the SWP practitioner to think more specifically about HR programme costs because these expenses typically account for the largest portion of overall workforce costs. What approach, then, should the SWP practitioner take to understand the particular HR programme-related expenses? A useful method to assess these costs is to start with a list of programmes that fall under the purview of the HR function. Typically, an HR function consists of some mix of the following sub-functions, teams or programmes:

- talent acquisition or recruiting;
- global mobility;
- compensation and benefits;
- learning and development;
- HR operations;
- employee relations;
- compliance;
- talent management:

- leadership development,
- succession planning,
- performance management;
- people analytics and SWP;
- safety.

With this list in hand, the SWP practitioner should engage with the leaders of each of these HR programmes in an attempt to better understand what some of the expected costs associated with these programmes might be. To that end, it is also a good idea to question these leaders on possible intangible costs that might impact on these programmes. These conversations should provide a good starting point for the SWP practitioner to think through where the organization might be spending money on its HR programmes, whether in the form of tangible or intangible costs.

Once the SWP practitioner has engaged with the relevant HR leaders regarding the HR programme spend, they should then reach out to their finance partner or partners who work directly on the HR budget for more detailed insight into how this money is being allocated across these programmes. The important thing for the SWP practitioner to remember is not to focus on an aggregate number that represents the cost of a particular HR programme, but rather to have the costs associated with the programme in question broken down on a per-employee basis. So, if the total budget for training and development is US $5 million and there are 2,000 employees in scope to receive training, the SWP practitioner should quickly realize that the organization will have a per-employee training spend of US $2,500. Where the per-employee spend approach becomes valuable is when the SWP practitioner factors in the future growth or retraction of the workforce. For example, if there are currently 2,000 employees in the organization that receive approximately US $2,500 a year in training each, what happens to the size of that budget when the workforce grows to 3,000 in the following year? Well, since the SWP practitioner knows the cost of training per employee, all they have to do is multiply this number by the projected workforce of 3,000. This calculation reveals the costs associated with training will grow to US $7.5 million – a substantial jump in the budget.

The preceding example demonstrates why it is imperative for the SWP practitioner to account for costs in the Strategic Workforce Plan. The per-employee training and development example only highlights one of many possible programmes that could be impacted by the company's projected growth. It is essential to think about what the total impact from a cost perspective would be if this activity was carried out across all of the HR programmes. It is easy to imagine how growing the workforce by 500 employees would stand to increase tangible workforce-related costs by tens of millions of dollars.

Including costs in the Strategic Workforce Plan

Accounting for costs in a Strategic Workforce Plan is important because it provides the SWP practitioner with a constraint to place on a plan that effectively acts as a limit that should not be exceeded when making strategic workforce-related decisions. Creating a Strategic Workforce Plan without cost constraints can severely restrict the usefulness of the plan. Why? Typically one of the primary purposes of creating a Strategic Workforce Plan is to build a more productive workforce. If the SWP practitioner works with business and HR leaders to create this plan, but does not include cost constraints in the plan, the output of the plan will probably suggest that the best approach to increase productivity would be to hire more employees, which in theory would lead to more production. For obvious reasons, if the company grossly overestimates the number of employees it should hire in an attempt to maximize productivity, but the cost of hiring those employees ends up being higher than the revenue generated by them, the company would be losing money. This is not an optimal outcome for any Strategic Workforce Plan.

Including costs in a Strategic Workforce Plan, however, provides the SWP practitioner with a methodology for building in the second key objective, which is to develop a workforce that is both efficient and effective. In other words, when the SWP practitioner is going through the activity of assessing the current versus the future state of the workforce and is developing a strategy to optimize that future

Figure 6.3   Example of a simple workforce decision-making cost-benefit analysis

workforce, they should be keeping these two concepts in mind. How do we develop a future workforce that is as equally productive as it is efficient? What are some tactics the SWP practitioner can leverage to develop a Strategic Workforce Plan that seeks to maximize both productivity and efficiency? One powerful method is to develop what-if scenarios and cost-benefit analyses that assess the trade-offs of pursuing different workforce-related strategies (see Figure 6.3). The key thing to remember here is the ability to develop diverse workforce-related scenarios and accurate cost-benefit analyses is contingent upon understanding the specific workforce-related costs that have been discussed throughout this chapter. With workforce-related costs in place, the SWP practitioner can begin to ask and answer questions such as:

- What is the incremental cost compared to the additional productivity gain of hiring one more employee?
- Will the productivity and costs associated with hiring that employee increase at the same rate or will one grow faster than the other?
- What can the organization do to ensure that productivity increases faster than the costs of hiring that employee?
- What is the trade-off between hiring a more junior employee who might be less productive or experienced but cost less compared to hiring a more experienced employee who might be more productive but substantially more expensive?

Although these questions are a tiny subset of the possible questions the SWP practitioner should be attempting to answer with the TCOW calculated as a factor in the Strategic Workforce Plan, they still illustrate the importance of accounting for these costs in that plan.

Summary of chapter objectives

Cost-based SWP

When it comes to organizational costs, there is usually a relatively clear relationship between a company's ability to manage its costs and success. This makes it important for the SWP practitioner to consider costs within the context of the broader Strategic Workforce Plan. The SWP practitioner should think of costs associated with workforce or HR programmes as constraints that the organization needs to factor in to get to an 'optimal' workforce state. When the final Strategic Workforce Plan is in place, there should be costs associated with all the forecasts and scenarios that account for factors such as headcount growth or retraction, location planning, training and development payroll and other workforce-related programmes. Assigning costs to all of these factors will give the SWP practitioner a baseline for assessing a metric known as the *total cost of the workforce* (TCOW).

The categories of workforce costs

Fixed costs

Put simply, a fixed cost is one that reoccurs at some fixed interval and is something that generally does not vary much regarding the amount of the cost that the company incurs. An example of a fixed cost is the cost associated with the salary a company pays to its salaried or exempt employees. A company is required to pay its salaried employees a fixed amount once or twice a month. An important aspect to understand regarding fixed costs is the company incurs them independently of any business impact or results that are realized because of those costs.

Variable costs

Variable costs are another form of cost that the SWP practitioner should consider when thinking through the types of workforce-related costs to account for in the final Strategic Workforce Plan. A variable cost, as opposed to a fixed cost, is a cost that changes depending on some circumstance in the business. Using salaried employees as an example, these employees receive a fixed amount of cash each pay period, regardless of what or how much they produce. For non-exempt (hourly) employees and commission-based employees, the same rule is not valid. In the case of these employees, the amount of cash they receive is dependent upon the amount of time they work and the number of sales they achieve.

Tangible costs

Any costs that are real and that the company is obligated to pay can be classified as a tangible cost. Moreover, these are costs that the company has to account for and report in its financial statements. Both fixed and variable costs are examples of tangible costs because they are costs that the firm actually incurs. Payroll, HRIS software, consulting support and learning and development software and licences are all examples of tangible costs related to the organiza-tion's people, HR and the SG&A budget.

Intangible costs

Intangible costs, as opposed to tangible costs, are costs that occur 'behind the scenes', but cannot necessarily be quantified. These costs typically are related to productivity and another form of cost known as an opportunity cost. An example of an intangible cost is the cost associated with having a workforce with low employee engagement. If an organization has a workforce lacking in engagement, it is likely that this low engagement, in turn, will lead to low productivity. The loss of productivity due to low engagement in the workforce is an example of an intangible cost. For obvious reasons, it is difficult to quantify from a financial perspective exactly how much the loss of productivity will cost the organization.

Opportunity costs

An opportunity cost is simply the cost of foregoing the benefits of one decision over another.

HR programme costs

Typically, an HR function consists of some mix of the following sub-functions, teams or programmes that each account for a significant workforce-related cost:

- talent acquisition or recruiting;
- global mobility;
- compensation and benefits;
- learning and development;
- HR operations;
- employee relations;
- compliance;
- talent management:
  - leadership development,
  - succession planning,
  - performance management;
- people analytics and SWP;
- safety.

Including costs in the Strategic Workforce Plan

Accounting for costs in a Strategic Workforce Plan is important because it provides the SWP practitioner with a constraint to place on a plan that effectively acts as a limit that should not be exceeded when making strategic workforce-related decisions. Creating a Strategic Workforce Plan without cost constraints can severely restrict the usefulness of the plan. Why? Typically one of the primary purposes of creating a Strategic Workforce Plan is to build a more productive workforce. If the SWP practitioner works with business and HR leaders to create this plan, but does not include cost constraints in the plan, the output of the plan would probably suggest that the best approach to increase productivity would be to hire more employees, which in theory would lead to more production. For obvious reasons, if the company grossly overestimates the number of employees it should hire in an attempt to maximize productivity, but the cost of hiring those employees ends up being higher than the revenue generated by them, the company will lose money. This is not an optimal outcome for any Strategic Workforce Plan.

Skills-based strategic workforce planning

Skills-based SWP

SWP is a valuable aspect of strategic HR and corporate strategy because it provides insights and answers to questions that HR and business leaders might have regarding how the future workforce should be structured to maximize company performance. Planning of this nature can answer questions such as:

- Where should corporate offices and facilities be located?
- How large should the workforce be?
- Is there an optimal mix of contingent versus FTEs?
- How much money should the organization allocate to learning and development to increase productivity?

Having an understanding of what the organization's actual head-count requirements will and should be in the future is crucial for being able to answer the above questions. Discussions in earlier chapters of this book have outlined the fact that gaining insight into headcount requirements is primarily a function of developing headcount supply and demand forecasts. Headcount requirements, however, are not the only component of the workforce on which the SWP practitioner should focus their attention. In fact, understanding headcount requirements probably makes up only half of the equation from an SWP standpoint. The other half of the equation involves understanding the impact of skills on the current and future workforce requirements. In this facet of SWP, the SWP practitioner is attempting to assess how skilled the workforce is at an aggregate level. They also are trying to understand where there are skills gaps in the workforce, which skills need more development and, finally, what skills the organization will require in the future that might not be in existence at the present time (see Figure 7.1).

Skills-based SWP is critical because it is the employee's proficiency at the skills required to complete the tasks associated with their jobs that drives the efficiency and productivity of the organization (Snell and Dean, 1992). As a hypothetical example, assume a technology company exists that relies heavily on software engineers to write code for the company's technology platform. The software engineers require certain programming skills to develop and improve the platform, which is at the core of the company's business model. Now, further assume this company just hired three software engineers who require proficiency in Java, C++ and Python to perform their duties in helping to build and enhance the company's software platform. If these three employees, however, are each only 33 per cent proficient at Java, C++ and Python, one could argue that, combined, these three employees are only as effective as one employee who possesses 100 per cent proficiency at these same skills. From a cost standpoint, the organization is paying three salaries but only actually receiving the 'full' talent of one employee. From this example, it is easy to see why it is so important for organizations to understand the skills level of the workforce in order to develop strategies to hire and retain employees that possess full proficiency in the skills that will contribute to the company's business model and strategy.

Figure 7.1 Skills-based SWP framework

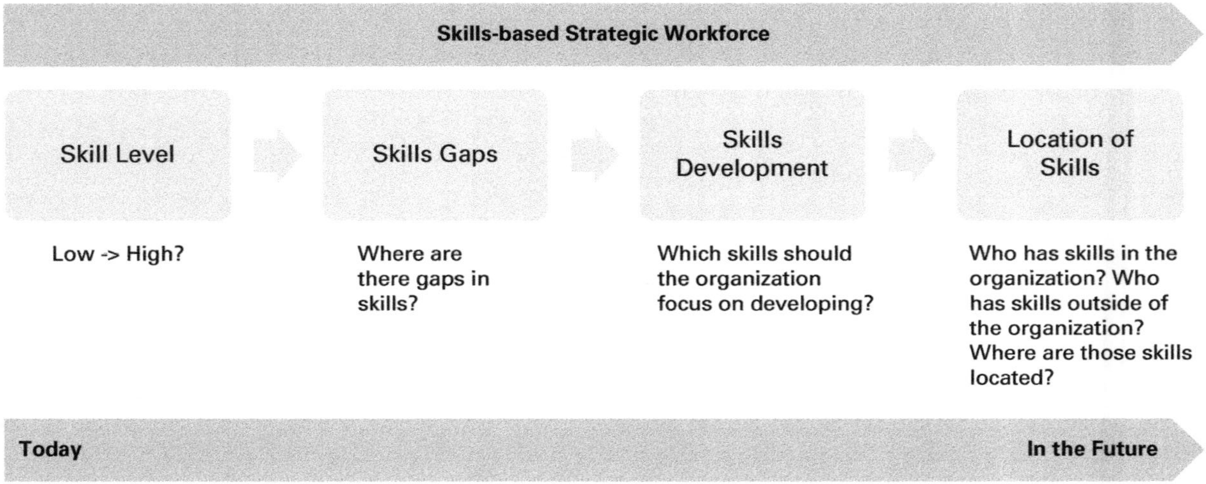

Skills-based Strategic Workforce

Skill Level

Low -> High?

Skills Gaps

Where are there gaps in skills?

Skills Development

Which skills should the organization focus on developing?

Location of Skills

Who has skills in the organization? Who has skills outside of the organization? Where are those skills located?

Today

In the Future

Skills-based SWP tends to be more of a priority for businesses that are more mature in nature with slower growth than for businesses in high-growth mode, where scaling the company's operations and business model through increasing the size of the workforce might be more of a priority. For businesses that are not growing and might even be retracting, the focus of SWP should be on maximizing the current workforce from an efficiency standpoint rather than trying to grow and scale the workforce. For these organizations, there is also a need to ensure that the individuals who are hired (usually due to backfill from attrition) are as skilled as or even more skilled than the current workforce and will contribute and build on the effectiveness currently in place.

The final component of skills-based SWP involves ensuring thought has been put into considering the future skills that the organization will require as technology changes and the company's business model matures. It is important to acknowledge that these 'future skills' might be skills that are available in the labour market, but have never been a requirement for the organization. Or, they can be skills that do not even exist either within or outside of the company. The fact that the company is trying to plan or anticipate what skills it will require in the future, while not fully knowing what will happen in that future, can be a daunting task. That said, it is still an activity or discussion the company should have in keeping with the theme of truly holistic SWP.

Assessing skills supply and demand

This section will review and elaborate on some of the strategies for assessing skills supply and demand that were discussed in Chapter 4 on talent supply. In order for an organization to maximize its productivity, it needs an efficient workforce. As illustrated in Figure 7.2, becoming efficient or 'optimized' happens when the workforce in question is sufficiently skilled and competent at executing the day-to-day activities essential for productivity (Koch and McGrath, 1996). So, how does an organization gain insight into how qualified, skilled and experienced its workforce is? Insight into the skills level of the organization can be gained by conducting a skills assessment (Duffy, 2001).

Figure 7.2   Creating productivity through an efficient workforce

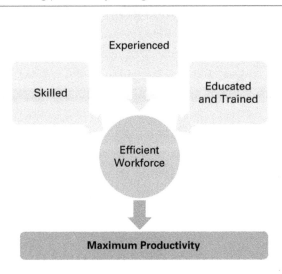

The ultimate objective in carrying out a skills assessment is to develop an inventory that allows the organization to look across the enterprise and assess how skilled, effective and proficient the workforce is regarding the key skills that the company builds its business model around. One aspect to recognize regarding a skills assessment is that each job or role in the organization will be likely to have several or even dozens of skills that may fall under the purview of that role. It is easy to see, then, why this activity can get complicated very quickly, which is why the roles in scope should be prioritized based on the critical workforce segments they fall under.

Another fact worth mentioning is that conducting a skills assessment is an activity that requires a significant amount of cross-functional collaboration between the organization's SWP team, HR department and the various business and team leaders. As mentioned earlier, because it can be a time-consuming exercise, it is good practice to begin the activity with the critical workforce segment or in the form of a pilot project. So, where to start? Before engaging in a full-blown, enterprise-wide, skills-assessment project, it makes sense to first take on a pilot project, preferably with the aforementioned critical workforce segment. From there, the following steps can provide a reliable roadmap of actions to take:

1 Identify which skills or jobs will be in scope for the skills inventory project.

2 Identify a manager, leader or small team that is knowledgeable on the requisite skills for the jobs that are in scope for the project.

3 Develop two separate surveys:

   a the first survey targets the manager who will rank each member of their team regarding their proficiency at the previously identified skill(s);

   b the second survey focuses on the individual employees rating their ability on the same skill set that the managers rated them on.

4 Multiply the total number of employees on the team involved in the analysis by the maximum proficiency score (which in this case is 10). For example, if 20 team members are required to have skill (X) then a fully proficient team would have a score of 200.

5 Have the team leader or manager conduct the skills ranking.

6 Aggregate the team leader's or manager's rankings across their entire team. For example, if there are 20 employees who all received a ranking of 7 for skill (X) the aggregate score would be 140.

7 Conduct the same activity in step six, but this time have the employees rank themselves.

8 Total the employee-level scores.

9 Average the employee-level scores and the manager-level scores.

10 Divide the averaged individual/manager scores by the maximum proficiency score to derive the skills proficiency level. For example, if the average manager/employee-level scores came out to 140, then the proficiency for the skill set in question would be $140/200 = 70$ per cent.

11 Repeat this process for the top skills that make up a particular job or role.

Once the SWP practitioner has worked with the principal HR and business leaders to complete the exercise, there should be a list in place of all the skills identified in the pilot project in rank order based on how 'skilled' or proficient the manager's employees are at each one. Understanding the skills-based proficiency level of employees at an aggregate level is invaluable information for HR and business leaders to have. A list of this nature will quickly provide these leaders with the knowledge they need to make decisions regarding how they develop the employees in their teams and in their organizations. It will also provide these leaders with additional data points for making major hiring decisions based on the skills that were identified as being deficient in the skills assessment activity.

Going through the exercise of conducting a skills inventory will be challenging but equally rewarding for the stakeholders involved. It will not only provide managers and HR leaders with the key insights discussed earlier, but also lay the foundation for building out a full inventory of skills across the organization. An inventory of skills of this nature is valuable because it opens the door for opportunities to use internal mobility not only for career development, but also as a lever to close some of the skills gaps that might be present in the organization.

Developing an internal skills inventory

What is an organizational skills inventory? Simply put, it is a catalogue of all the skills an organization (or a team or department in an organization) possesses to accomplish the day-to-day tasks related to that organization's strategy and business model (see Figure 7.3). Combining

Figure 7.3   Skills inventory framework

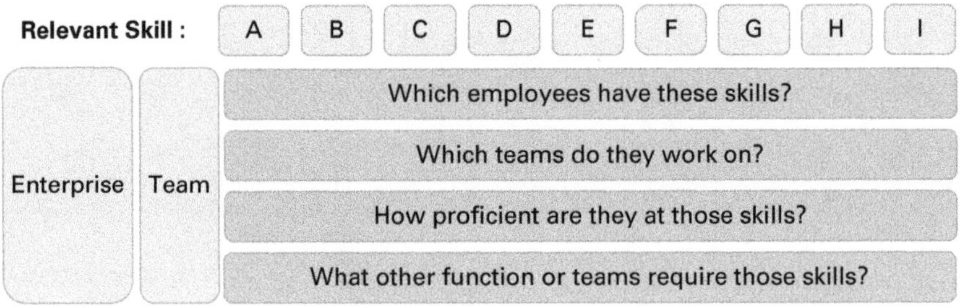

the skills inventory with the output from the skills assessment activity should provide business leaders with a comprehensive list of all the skills in the organization, how proficient employees are at those skills, and which teams and functions across the firm possess those skills. Incorporating the skills assessment outputs into the skills inventory also will provide business leaders and managers with insight into which teams, departments and functions have higher or lower levels of proficiency in the skill sets critical to the organization's mission. This level of insight is useful from a developmental and training aspect too, where managers can potentially leverage the teams with higher skills levels to train teams with lower skills levels. Understanding skill proficiency levels across teams also can lead to opportunities to study teams that are more proficient in certain skills in order to understand and possibly replicate the factors, circumstances or environments that have led to this skills divide between the teams.

Finally, and perhaps most importantly, possessing a full inventory of skills across the enterprise opens the door to possibly filling the skills gaps that exist in certain roles or pockets of the organization with employees from other parts of the organization who might possess those skills. An inventory of skills then becomes extremely useful in instances where managers might traditionally look to recruit external candidates to fill skills gaps in their teams. With an inventory of skills visible across the enterprise, these managers now can fill the skills void with the organization's own internal employees. Filling roles internally not only provides more career opportunities for existing employees, but also reduces recruiting costs and cuts down on the risk of hiring an external candidate who might not be a good cultural fit for the team or company.

Before an inventory of skills can become useful to the business leaders and the organization, the skills have to be captured and catalogued in such a way that managers have visibility and access to the repository of skills that have been captured. To do this effectively requires cross-functional collaboration and significant upfront planning between the organization's SWP function, business leaders and HR. Planning how the organization will publish and make the inventory of skills available to these key stakeholders can be accomplished by asking and answering a series of questions:

- What team and individual in the organization will be responsible for owning the skills inventory?
- How often will the skills inventory be reviewed?
- How often will the skills inventory be updated?
- Will the skills inventory be part of the SWP process?
- Will the skills inventory be for all roles across the organization or only for roles/skills that fall into critical workforce segments?
- What technology will be used to catalogue the inventory of skills (eg Excel or a customized field in the organization's HRIS)?
- How will managers and business leaders access the inventory of skills?
- Will talent acquisition have access to the skills inventory for recruiting purposes?
- In addition to talent acquisition, what other stakeholders should have access to the inventory of skills?
- Should employees be provided with access to the inventory of skills to gain insight into possible career opportunities?

Once these questions have been answered, the SWP practitioner, key business leaders and HR should begin the process of developing a roadmap for a roll-out and implementation of the skills inventory project. The implementation roadmap should outline:

- a definitive timeline for the project to be implemented;
- key actions required at different phases of the project;
- if the project will be enterprise-wide or a critical workforce segment pilot;
- clearly defined roles and responsibilities along with measures of accountability;
- executive sponsorship;
- milestones;
- success metrics;
- clearly outlined processes and interdependencies;
- communication and change-management strategy.

Assessing future skills requirements

As was discussed in Chapter 4, one of the most challenging aspects of skills-based SWP is planning for the skills that the company will be likely to require in the future, but are not in existence in the organization today. The challenge here is that companies evolve and business models change to adapt to external factors, such as increased competition and changing technologies. Changes to an organization's business model usually lead to accompanying changes in the requirements for the skills that are needed to execute on the strategic objectives that have evolved with the changing of those business models. All of these factors lead to the importance of the SWP practitioner accounting for the possibility of introducing new skills requirements into the organization for the evolution of the company's business model. From a practical standpoint, it makes sense to break down future skills requirements into short, medium and long-term requirements. There also should be some acknowledgement of the fact that the further into the future the organization plans for these skills, the less certainty there will be regarding the particular skill set of requirements the company will need. Regarding future skills requirements, there are two levels of complexity that the SWP practitioner should consider when evaluating the future demand for these skills.

Skills not available in the external market

The first level deals with the skills currently in existence in the external market, but not currently in use in the organization's day-to-day operations. Determining these skills requirements is usually a function of having a solid understanding of the organization's current business model along with an equally solid understanding of the external forces that are shaping the industry in which the company competes. If the SWP practitioner partners with business leaders to understand these factors, there is a good chance they will be able to identify the types of skills the company will require in the future.

Skills not in existence

The second level of complexity deals with skills that are not used in the organization and do not exist in the external market either. The requirements for these skills are usually long term in nature and typically deal with changes in technology that could potentially revamp the industry in which the company competes. These could be technologies like artificial intelligence, machine learning and quantum computing.

So, how should the SWP practitioner assess the future skills requirements for the organization? The short answer to this question is that the SWP practitioner should engage in an activity that involves a degree of out-of-the-box thinking and cross-functional partnership. As was discussed in the talent supply chapter, think of this activity as being equal parts brainstorming and equal parts crystal ball forecasting. Although by no means a precise activity, the SWP practitioner should develop a series of questions to work through with these cross-functional partners with the intention of bringing more focus to the brainstorming sessions. Some questions that might be useful to stimulate this discussion include:

- What are the technological trends in the industry or sector in which our organization competes?
- Are technological advances going to complicate or simplify the way in which the organization conducts its work?
- If future technology is likely to require new skills, what might those skills be:
    - people-facing, sales or customer-service skills?
    - maths or science skills?
    - computer programming and engineering skills?
    - trade skills, such as welders?
    - physical labour?
    - leadership skills?
    - cultural adaptability or language skills?
    - logistics skills (pilots, bus drivers or truck drivers)?

Once the list of future skills is complete, the SWP practitioner should work with these same business and HR leaders to assign a series of probabilities to each skill based on the likelihood of the organization requiring that skill. These probabilities should be part of a timeline that outlines when the organization might require the skills. From this activity, the SWP practitioner can develop scenarios regarding the possibility of the organization legitimately requiring the skills along with starting to explore the external labour market for the availability of those skills.

Summary of chapter objectives

Skills-based SWP

Understanding headcount forecasts and requirements is an important part of SWP; however, it is not the only component of the workforce that the SWP practitioner should focus on. In fact, understanding headcount requirements probably makes up only half of the equation from an SWP standpoint. The other half of the SWP equation is understanding the impact of skills on the current and future workforce requirements. In this component of SWP, the SWP practitioner is attempting to assess how skilled the workforce is at an aggregate level. They also are trying to understand where there are skills gaps in the workforce, which skills need more development and, finally, what skills the organization will require in the future.

A framework for assessing skills supply and demand

In order for an organization to maximize its productivity, it needs an efficient workforce. Becoming efficient or 'optimized' happens when the workforce is fully skilled and competent at executing the day-to-day activities essential for productivity. So, how does an organization gain insight into how qualified, skilled and experienced its workforce is? Answer: by conducting a skills assessment. The ultimate objective in conducting a skills assessment is to develop an inventory that allows the organization to look across the enterprise to assess how skilled, effective and proficient the workforce is regarding the key skills the company needs to execute on its strategy. One key aspect to recognize regarding a skills assessment is the fact that each job or role in the organization will be likely to have several or even dozens of skills required by that role.

The process involved in creating an organizational skills inventory

Creating an organizational skills inventory involves cataloguing of all the skills an organization (or a team or department in an organization) possesses to accomplish the day-to-day tasks related to that organization's strategy and business model. Combining the skills inventory with the output from the skills assessment activity should provide business leaders with a comprehensive list of all the skills in the organization, how proficient employees are at those skills, and which teams and functions across the firm possess these skills. Incorporating the skills assessment outputs into the skills inventory also will provide business leaders and managers with insight into which teams, departments and functions have higher or lower levels of proficiency with these skill sets. This level of insight is useful from a developmental and training aspect too, where managers potentially can leverage the teams with higher skills levels to train the teams with lower skills levels.

A framework for assessing future skills requirements

There are two components involved in determining future skills requirements for the organization. Each of these components deals with a different level of complexity. The first component involves assessing future skills currently in existence in the external market, but not currently in use in the organization's day-to-day operations. Determining these skills requirements is usually a function of having a solid understanding of the organization's current business model along with an equally solid understanding of the external forces that are shaping the industry in which that company competes.

The second component with a higher level of complexity deals with determining future skills that are not used in the organization and do not exist in the external market either. The requirements for these skills are usually long term in nature and typically deal with changes in technology that could potentially revamp the industry in which the company competes. These could be technologies like artificial intelligence, machine learning and quantum computing. To assess future skills, the SWP practitioner should engage in a brainstorming activity with HR and business leaders that seeks to answer the following questions:

- What are the technological trends in the industry or sector in which our organization competes?
- Are technological advances going to complicate or simplify the way in which the organization conducts its work?
- If future technology is likely to require new skills, what might those skills be:
  - people-facing, sales or customer-service skills?
  - maths or science skills?
  - computer programming and engineering skills?
  - trades skills such as welders?
  - physical labour?
  - leadership skills?
  - cultural adaptability or language skills?
  - logistics skills (pilots, bus drivers or truck drivers)?

Skills-based SWP is critical in the SWP process because it is the employee's proficiency at the skills required to complete the tasks associated with their jobs that drives the efficiency and productivity of the organization. Skills-based SWP tends to be more of a priority for businesses that are more mature in nature with slower growth than for businesses in high-growth mode, where scaling the company's operations and business model through increasing the size of the workforce is more of a priority. For companies that are not growing and might even be retracting, the focus of SWP should be on maximizing the current workforce from an efficiency standpoint. For these organizations, there is also a need to ensure that the individuals who are hired (usually due to backfill from attrition) are as skilled or even more skilled than the current workforce and will contribute and build on the effectiveness that is currently in place within the organization. The remainder of the book will continue to touch upon and highlight the importance of understanding skills as they relate to the organization's current and future strategic objectives.

Strategic workforce planning for location strategy

08

CHAPTER OBJECTIVES

1 Describe the link between SWP and location and site selection.
2 Describe how location strategies can be used to attract and retain talent.
3 Describe a framework to create location and site-selection criteria.
4 Outline how to analyse current versus future location and site requirements.
5 Describe how to optimize space planning to improve the employee experience.

SWP and location selection

There are various reasons why a company might choose a particular site, location, region or country in the world in which to build an office and establish a market presence. Irrespective of the strategic business reasons for a company doing this, the ability to attract, retain and develop key talent invariably will be a factor that plays a role in that location's success or failure within the organization's broader corporate strategy. SWP can and should play a significant role in helping the organization's business leaders think through how the talent and workforce associated with that location can impact on the ability for the location to be successful in the company's longer-term strategic objectives. More specifically, SWP can help to inform location decisions by providing insight into a variety of factors. A few of these factors include:

- talent supply and availability in the location's market;
- FTE and contingent employee growth forecasts for the location;
- competitor talent intelligence in location space-planning optimization for positive employee experience at the location;
- current and future state talent scenario analysis;
- quality of life and cost of living information for the location.

There is little doubt that, when a company selects a new site or location in which to establish a presence, there is likely to have been a significant amount of thought put into the decision – at least from a business perspective. Unfortunately, many organizations over index on the business component of this decision and fail to think through in sufficient detail how the employees working at that site can potentially contribute to the location's success or failure. Introducing SWP into the site-selection process ensures that the organization is thinking as strategically about the employee contribution to the success or failure of the location as they are thinking strategically about the business factors that could impact on its success or failure (Figure 8.1).

Figure 8.1   Location selection information provided by SWP

Location strategies to attract and retain talent

Typically, when an organization makes the decision to develop offices, plants or factories in a new region, city or location, the reason for this relates to some aspect of the company's long-term strategy. In these instances, talent may and should be one of the prime factors involved in the final decision regarding where the new site should be located. That said, business factors are not always the primary reason why companies choose new sites and locations for their operations. As the competitive landscape in businesses and industries around the world intensifies, talent as a differentiator and competitive advantage has become a foundational pillar for the strategies of many organizations. In these situations, companies will often choose locations based strictly on that location's ability to help the company attract and retain top talent. These companies see a prime location as a way to build on their employer brand offering to attract candidates that might otherwise not be interested in working for that company. When this is the case, the SWP practitioner needs to work with business leaders and site-selection decision makers to think through and develop location-based strategies that will accomplish the goal of attracting and retaining that top talent. One might be inclined to ask why this is the role of the SWP practitioner, to which the response is three-fold. First, the decision regarding the new location is a strategic decision (the first word in SWP is 'strategic'). Second, the decision regarding the new location is typically centred around optimizing or improving some aspect of the workforce. Third, the decision will require internal and external market data and analysis. From these three factors, there is no individual or team better suited for the task than the SWP practitioner and their accompanying team.

When considering a new location strategy to attract and retain talent, the first question the SWP practitioner is likely to ask is: where to start? A good starting point is to gain a better understanding of the demographics being targeted for the site from a talent perspective. If the SWP practitioner is to conduct an assessment of the feasibility of one location over another, they will first need to understand some essential characteristics about the demographic the organization is attempting to attract and retain with its new location strategy. This initial question should lead to a series of clarifying questions that should help to provide directional guidance from which to start a formal location feasibility assessment. To that end, some fundamental questions that the SWP practitioner should be asking include:

- What workforce segment or segments is the organization targeting from an attraction and retention standpoint?
- What skill sets do potential candidates and current employees in this workforce segment possess?
- Are there higher concentrations of these skill sets in certain cities, regions or countries around the world? If yes, why?
- What are the generational characteristics that the workforce segment being targeted possesses? For example, millennials versus baby-boomers?
- From an educational standpoint, are there common characteristics that members of the workforce segment in question share?

As it relates to the organization's location strategy, answers to these questions can shed light on the types of cities, regions or general areas that the workforce segment being targeted might find most appealing. For example, the organization may have identified a highly technical workforce segment made up of millennials as being the focus area for its workforce location strategy. The SWP practitioner could do some basic research that might reveal recent trends in millennial migration patterns suggest that millennials tend to migrate towards and enjoy living in larger urban areas or cities such as New York, San Francisco, London, Tokyo or Singapore. Putting the technical skills lens on the same analysis might further reveal that highly technical millennials might not only migrate to large urban areas but also locations with other technically savvy millennials, such as London, Boston or San Francisco.

The above example is just the start of the analysis. Once answers are in place for the demographic questions, the SWP practitioner should shift their focus to understanding factors within the specific locations that could provide insight into the potential for long and short-term sustainability for this location. In this component of the analysis the focus transforms from lifestyle and quality of life factors that might be appealing to the specific workforce segment, to ensuring that the location will lead to positive outcomes for both the employees being targeted and the business decision behind the location strategy. Questions to ask for clarity on this component include:

- What is the quantified assessment of the talent supply being targeted for the new location?
- What are the urban or suburban trends relating to the supply of talent for the location? In other words, is talent supply flowing into or out of the particular areas being analysed?
- What do cost of living, the housing market and other macroeconomic variables look like for the location? Are there positive or negative trends that could potentially impact on the location strategy's ability to attract and retain talent?

The final component of the analysis includes conducting a cost-benefit assessment of the location. In this part of the analysis, the SWP practitioner is taking a step back to factor in the cost of the new location relative to the positive impact the company is hoping to gain from the new site. In other words, if a suitable site has been identified that will contribute to attracting and retaining top talent, but the cost of operating an office at that site is so expensive that it negates the benefits, from a cost perspective, of attracting and retaining top talent, the organization might want to look at alternative sites that are less expensive.

Developing selection criteria for a new location

Companies around the world operate in a variety of locations across the globe for a host of different reasons. The factors that led these organizations to choose one specific site over another also vary dramatically. Some companies might develop location strategies with the intention of penetrating into new markets, while others might create strategies to minimize costs or to gain access to skilled talent pools. GameStop is a good example of a small retail box store in the United States, which competes in a market with much larger box-store companies such as Walmart, Target and Best Buy, that has been able to use a location strategy to remain competitive. Moreover, GameStop uses four distinct strategies to penetrate new markets and compete with the aforementioned big-box retailers. The first three strategies are: product pricing, product differentiation and customer service; the fourth and final tactic used, however, is a location strategy that targets certain geographies where the company might be more likely to succeed and gain a larger market share. This strategy has been highly effective for GameStop in its ability to remain competitive and steadily chip away at the market share of those big-box retailers (Schrantz, 2013).

Whatever the drivers of a location strategy may be, there should be significant upfront thought put into developing a methodology for comparing and assessing locations. One simple methodological approach is to develop a list of criteria with which to rank locations. The SWP practitioner should be involved in helping the site-selection leaders and decision makers think through the people or workforce component criteria of the decision-making process. Depending on the organization, there will always be certain nuances in terms of the importance and priority of the workforce criteria that the organization should consider when making strategic location decisions. Despite these nuances, there are some fairly common themes that most organizations should consider when developing the workforce criteria for a strategic location decision.

Available talent

The first workforce factor to consider is whether or not there is a labour market in the location the organization is considering that will support the company's goals. A location that has an abundant supply of local talent from which the organization can source quality candidates always will be more attractive than a location with a limited supply of 'good' talent.

Quality of living

The next workforce-related factor is the quality of life in the area being considered. Here the SWP practitioner is trying to determine if potential candidates will want to move to the new location. Also, if they are already living in the location, will they want to stay? In other words, are there local factors that are diminishing the attractiveness of the site or are there factors making it more attractive?

Cost of living

Assessing the cost of living for the locations being considered is also a fundamental criteria to include in the final assessment. The objective of incorporating this component in the criteria is that it will provide the organization with some high-level insight regarding whether or not the company's current pay structure can support the location being evaluated. Here the question becomes: does the organization have the budget to pay employees enough to live in the location under consideration? There are numerous resources available online to compare the cost of living for various cities and locations around the world. These online resources include: numbeo.com, bankrate.com and swz.salary.com. When reviewing these sources of information, it is important to ensure that they include variables such as housing and rent, cost of a bundle of goods, fuel, transportation and entertainment in the final index.

Geographical location of the site

The actual geographical location of the site also should be on the list of criteria the company considers. This criteria is intended to assess whether the geographical location relative to other locations is positive or negative. Questions to consider might be:

- Is the location isolated or close to other major metro areas?
- How easy is it to fly into and out of the site?
- Are there time-zone considerations that might make the site less desirable?
- What is the climate like at the location?
- Is the climate more or less attractive than at other sites?

Location infrastructure

The infrastructure at the location is also a factor that should be considered in the selection of key criteria. Questions concerning the location's infrastructure include:

- How will the location's infrastructure impact on employees' commute times?
- Are traffic problems and over congestion issues that could impact on the attractiveness of the location for potential candidates?
- What does public transport look like at the location?
- Is it convenient or more time consuming to use public transport?
- Is infrastructure improving or diminishing at the location?
- Is there adequate housing?
- What are crime rates at the location?
- Will potential employees feel safe living and working in the location?

Immigration

Many organizations, especially larger global organizations, rely heavily on international talent to meet the demand for the organization's skills requirements. For companies that do rely heavily on international talent, including the host country's immigration policy as part of the criteria for evaluation is very important. Here the SWP practitioner should be thinking through questions such as:

- How easy will it be for international candidates to receive working visas?
- How long does the visa process take?
- How international is the location?
- Will international candidates feel alienated or welcomed at the site?

Developing and evaluating potential locations against a set of workforce-related criteria as part of the broader site-selection process is critical and should be considered a key aspect of any site-selection

Figure 8.2   Key location selection criteria to consider when selecting a new site

decision (see Figure 8.2). Ensuring that these workforce-related factors have been accounted for in the final decision will provide leaders with confidence in knowing that all of the variables that could potentially impact on the success of that site – from a workforce standpoint – were analysed and evaluated thoroughly.

Analysing current versus future location and site requirements

A recurring theme in SWP involves understanding how the landscape of the current workforce will change in the future as the company evolves. This theme holds true in the context of planning for a location strategy as well. Fundamentally, the SWP practitioner should be helping the organization think through how the current requirements for a site-selection decision might change over time. Bringing this information to the decision-making discussion will provide more insight for leaders concerning the long-term sustainability of the locations that are being evaluated. When analysing the current versus future requirements for a location strategy, the organization should consider three crucial factors: employee demographics, corporate strategy and macroeconomic variables.

Employee demographics

Regarding the workforce component of a location strategy, the demographics of the workforce are an integral element of the strategy that should be on leaders' radars as the SWP practitioner works with these leaders to identify aspects of the workforce that should be included in the final location decision. Understanding the demographics of the workforce is so important that it makes sense for the SWP practitioner to think about how these demographics could impact on the success of the site in the current state. This holds true not only for the current state but also for how changes in the demographics might impact on the success of the site in the future. Assessing the impact of demographics on a site in the current versus future state involves asking the following questions:

- Are impending retirements an issue with the current workforce?
- Will the backfills for retirements be filled by a particular generational employee profile, eg millennials, or will the backfill be distributed across multiple generations?
- Is the workforce composed of younger millennials? If so, will the site be as appealing to this generation as they grow older and start families?
- Is the current workforce primarily international?
- Does the organization source global employees because there is a lack of skills in the company's domestic market? If so, will this trend hold true in the future – meaning will key skills always be sourced internationally or will these skills be available in the organization's domestic market one day?
- Will the talent landscape from where the organization sources key skills change?

- Will there be new talent 'hot spots' around the world that might impact on the ability to source key talent at the chosen location?

- Many organizations are placing more importance on diversity strategies. Will the organization's diversity strategy impact on the attractiveness of the final location selected – meaning is it located in a market that lends itself to a diverse talent pool?

Corporate strategy

For obvious reasons, it is crucial for the SWP practitioner to think about how the long-term corporate strategy could impact on both the location strategy and the workforce that ultimately ends up working at that new location. The important area to focus on when thinking about the corporate strategy's potential impact on the location strategy (from a workforce standpoint) is how the evolution of that strategy might change the skills or jobs that the organization might require. If these skills are substantially different from the skills currently in place, and hence require an entirely different employee profile for the future, the SWP practitioner needs to factor this into whether the sites up for consideration will be flexible enough to accommodate these new skills requirements. A useful way to approach this situation is to analyse the comprehensiveness of the talent pool for each location up for consideration. Questions that should be answered in this analysis include:

- How many and what types of universities and post-secondary educational institutions are located in the area being evaluated? Are these universities famous for any specific academic programmes?

- Is the area a talent hotspot for a particular skill set, eg London for finance or Silicon Valley for technology?

- Is there one dominant industry in the city or location that is being considered or does the local market support multiple industries?

- What are the major companies that operate out of the location? Are they competitors?

- Is the location growing and attracting more talent or shrinking and seeing an exodus of talent?

In addition to thinking about how the corporate strategy could impact on the requirement for skills and new jobs, the SWP practitioner also should be assessing where the company is in its life cycle:

- Is the company growing, shrinking or remaining static in terms of headcount requirements?
- Is the company testing new products and markets that could lead to future growth?
- Is the company broadening or consolidating its service or product offering?

Assessing how the evolution of the corporate strategy could potentially impact on the workforce requirements for that location will ensure the workforce component of the location strategy is in alignment with the company's broader corporate objectives.

Macroeconomic factors

The final aspect of the current versus future state assessment deals with analysing what the potential impact on the location's success might be if local economic factors change. In this part of the analysis, the SWP practitioner should be looking for certain trends in the local economies at the sites that are in the scope of the new location. In addition to identifying trends in these local markets, the SWP practitioner also should be looking to understand the underlying factors that are driving the trend up or down. Finally, the SWP practitioner should be thinking about how the economic trends they are assessing might impact on the workforce at the new location. Some of the key local economic factors that should be analysed include:

- *Job growth:* Is employment growing, shrinking or remaining static? How does this job growth compare across locations and against the national average?
- *Migration patterns:* Are people moving to or from the city or location? What is driving these migration patterns?
- *Fiscal health:* Is the location fiscally healthy? Does the city or location consistently operate under a budget deficit? Is that deficit growing or shrinking?

- *Housing:* Are new houses being built? Is there a surplus or shortage of housing? Is the surplus or shortage growing or shrinking? Are the migration patterns mentioned earlier driving growth or contraction in the housing market or is it the other way around?

- *Taxes:* How do the tax rates compare across the different locations? Have taxes increased, decreased or remained static? What is driving the increase or decrease in tax rates?

Once the SWP practitioner has carefully analysed each location across these key areas and can confidently answer each of the preceding questions, the results should be ranked and summarized based on the potential positive or negative impact those factors could have on the workforce and locations being analysed.

New location space planning

Identifying a suitable location in which to build a new site should not be the end of the SWP practitioner's involvement in the organization's site strategy. Once the full location feasibility assessment is complete, the SWP practitioner should shift focus to providing input to the organization's facilities design team on the development of an optimal space in which employees can work. In recent years, increasingly more organizations have turned to more comfortable, customized and elaborate workplace designs, in the hopes of increasing productivity, collaboration and creativity (Leblebici, 2012). As in the site-selection process, the SWP practitioner can provide valuable research and insight into how a workspace should be designed to provide maximum utility for the targeted workforce.

For the space-planning analysis, the SWP practitioner should take a similar approach to that used in the site-selection process to gain insight into how the new location's targeted workforce might respond to different workspace designs, perks and technology. From a workforce standpoint, there are three key aspects to the space design that the SWP practitioner should consider: employee workspace expectations, workspace productivity and technology in the workspace.

Employee workspace expectations

There was a time in the not too distant past when the design, functionality and amenities that a workspace provided to employees were much less important to these employees than the notion of just having a stable job to go to everyday. Like virtually everything in life, however, things change, progress moves forward, and expectations evolve. The maturation of the modern workspace is no different. So, what is the driving factor behind the evolution of the workspace in recent years? A major factor of some of the most popular trends in workspace strategies in the last few years is the change in demographics that make up the workforce for many organizations. A large volume of baby-boomers are retiring every day and are being replaced by a younger workforce, often millennials, that have entirely different expectations regarding their day-to-day workspace experience. For example, in the fourth quarter of 2016 over 800,000 Americans over the age of 65 without disabilities left the workforce (Kawa, 2017).

The SWP practitioner should be providing the facilities and workspace design teams with information regarding the demographics and profiles of the employees that will be working in these spaces. Doing so will give context on how space should be designed to maximize the aforementioned productivity, engagement, collaboration and creativity. If the SWP practitioner was involved in the site-selection process, they should have significant insight into these employee demographics and profiles. To that end, the questions the SWP practitioner should seek to answer include:

- What will be the age distribution of the workforce that will occupy the space? For example, will 50–70 per cent of the workforce be under the age of 30?
- How will this age distribution change over time?
- What type of work will take place on a day-to-day basis at the site: sales, computer programming, factory work etc?
- From where will the employees working at the new site come? Will they be current employees who will transfer? Are they coming from competitors? Are they coming from international destinations?

So, how will the questions above impact the employees' expectations of their workspace? If they are coming from a technology company in Silicon Valley, their expectations are likely to be much different than if they are coming from an automobile factory in Detroit.

Workspace productivity

Once the facilities and space design team have a firm grasp on the type of employees that will occupy the workspace, the SWP practitioner can work with this team to identify factors – from a workspace standpoint – that might contribute to a more productive and satisfied workforce (see Figure 8.3). A few factors to include when developing a workspace strategy are productivity, collaboration, comfort and creativity (Vischer, 2012).

Figure 8.3 Workspace design consideration process

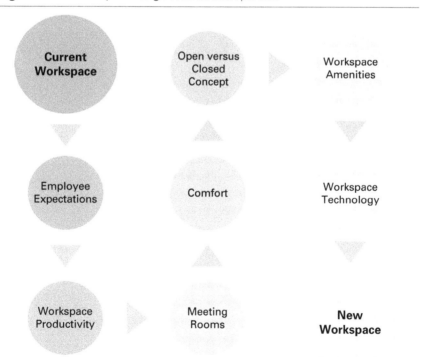

Open versus closed concept

An open concept where everyone sits in an open space can lead to information flowing much more freely. It can also lead to more collaboration and stronger relationships across teams. The downside to this approach is that some employees may find this form of work environment noisy, chaotic and distracting, which potentially can lead to a decrease in productivity compared to a closed concept (Kim and de Dear, 2013). An open-concept work design might be especially distracting for employees that come from a more traditional workspace. If this is the route the organization chooses, it should provide employees with noise-cancelling headsets to ensure they are still able to maintain their productivity.

Comfort

Ensuring employees are working in a workspace that is comfortable can go a long way towards creating a productive and engaged workforce. When optimizing for comfort, space should be designed with lighting, sounds and smells conducive to fostering relaxation and focus (Vischer, 2012). If the organization decides on an open-concept workspace, there should be plenty of room for employees to move freely and 'get away' from the buzz of day-to-day activity if they so desire.

Meeting rooms

How does the organization like to conduct meetings? Do meetings normally contain a large number of participants or are they smaller and more focused? Is the company trying to move to a culture of more productive meetings? If so, thought should be put into how to design meeting rooms to meet this criterion. Should there be a large number of small meeting rooms or several large meeting rooms? Should these rooms be formal or more relaxed and free flowing? Answers to these questions once again will be dependent upon the profiles of the employees that occupy the workspace along with the culture the organization is striving to achieve.

Workspace amenities

Once again depending on the demographics, industry and competitors of the organization (not to mention budget), the amenities the company provides within the workspace have the potential to impact on the employee experience significantly. Typically, from an employee perspective, the more amenities that are available in the workspace, the more attractive that workspace becomes (Earle, 2003). The types of amenities an organization can potentially provide for employees in the workspace are vast. Many contemporary organizations in Silicon Valley offer everything imaginable to their employees. Perks that these organizations offer include everything from on-site valet parking to free meals, dry cleaning and gym facilities. It is important to note, however, that perks do not always have to be as elaborate as those offered by large technology companies. Smaller perks such as offering coffee and small snacks can still lead to positive benefits in attracting and retaining employees and should be considered an alternative for smaller companies that do not have the resources to offer elaborate on-site perks.

Providing workspace perks to employees is an aspect of an organization's location strategy that should be considered and analysed carefully. On the one hand, delivering comprehensive perks to employees can get very expensive very quickly. On the other hand, the potential upside benefit of offering these perks can be substantial. Providing extensive workspace amenities can be a differentiator for the organization's talent brand. It can lead to a more satisfied workforce and, frankly speaking, many younger workers expect certain core amenities to be available to them in their workspace. It should be the job of the SWP practitioner to analyse the cost versus benefits of these amenities and help to inform senior leaders on how comprehensive the amenities offerings should be at the new site.

Workspace technology

Technology is the final component that should be a discussion point when developing and designing a workspace to optimize the employee experience for productivity, engagement, collaboration and creativity. Like the other factors under consideration in the workplace design strategy, the technological approach to the workspace will be dependent on the profile of the employees occupying the workplace along with the type of work they will be doing. In addition to these two factors, the organization's available budget for the site also will be a factor that contributes to the final workplace technology strategy. The SWP practitioner should provide specific information to the workplace strategy decision makers by helping to answer the following questions:

- Will the day-to-day activities at the new site require different technology than what is currently in place at the organization's other locations?

- Will the employees who work at the new site be more or less technically savvy than at other sites across the organization?

- How can technology be used to support other aspects of the broader workplace strategy. For example, if the organization opts for an open-space concept for the new site, should employees have access to noise-cancelling headphones to reduce distractions?

- How can technology be leveraged to improve productivity by increasing the convenience of being at work? Ideas to increase productivity and convenience include:

  - on-site tech support kiosks where employees can get technology-related questions and support answered in real time;

  - vending machines where employees can go to gain immediate access to small technology items such as a computer mouse, phone charger or privacy screen;

  - meeting-scheduling software designed to make booking meetings easier.

- Will the new location require heavy interaction with other locations around the world? If so, can enhanced video-conferencing improve this experience?

- Are there trends in future technology, such as virtual reality, that could be game changers regarding employees interacting with each other and could be a pilot for the new site in the future?

Developing and optimizing a workplace to drive productivity, employee engagement, collaboration and creativity requires careful thought and a significant amount of data to make an informed decision. The SWP function is uniquely positioned to be the perfect partner in helping the facilities design team and all decision makers involved think through the workforce-related factors that can inform these decisions and should be actively involved in the end-to-end process from day one.

Summary of chapter objectives

The link between SWP and location and site selection

There are various reasons why a company might choose a particular site, location, region or country in the world to build an office and establish a market presence. Irrespective of the strategic business reasons for a company doing this, the ability to attract, retain and develop key talent invariably will be a factor that plays a role in that location's success or failure within the organization's broader corporate strategy. SWP can and should play a significant part in helping the organization's business leaders think through how the talent and workforce associated with that location can impact on its ability to become a successful component of the company's longer-term strategic objectives. More specifically, SWP can help to inform location decisions by providing insight into a variety of factors. A few of these factors include:

- talent supply and availability in the location's market;
- FTE and contingent employee growth forecasts for the location;
- competitor talent intelligence in the location space planning optimization for positive employee experience at the location;
- current and future state talent scenario analysis;
- quality of life and cost of living information for the location.

How location strategies can be used to attract and retain talent

Business factors are not always the primary reason for companies choosing new sites and locations for their operations. As the competitive landscape in businesses and industries around the world intensifies, talent as a differentiator and competitive advantage has become a foundational pillar in the strategies of many organizations. In these situations, companies will often choose locations based strictly on a location's ability to help the company attract and retain top talent. These companies see a prime location as a way to build on their employer brand offering to candidates who otherwise might not be interested in working for that company.

Framework to create location and site-selection criteria

Developing criteria against which to assess the different locations is important. The SWP practitioner should be involved in helping the site-selection leaders and decision makers think through the people or workforce component criteria of the decision-making process. Depending on the organization, there will always be certain nuances in the importance and priority of the workforce criteria that the organization should consider when making strategic location decisions. Despite these nuances, there are some fairly common themes that most organizations should consider when developing the workforce criteria for making a strategic location decision. Critical criteria to include are:

- quality of life factors;
- cost of living factors;
- geographical location of the sites;
- infrastructure factors;
- immigration policies.

Analysing current versus future location and site requirements

Regarding the assessment of the current versus future site requirements, the SWP practitioner should be helping the organization to think through how the current requirements for a site-selection decision might change over time. Bringing this information to the decision-making discussion will provide more insight for leaders concerning the long-term sustainability of the locations that are being evaluated. When analysing the current versus future requirements for a location strategy, the organization should consider three crucial factors: employee demographics, corporate strategy and macroeconomic variables.

Optimizing space planning to improve the employee experience

Identifying a suitable location in which to build a new site should not be the end of the SWP practitioner's involvement in the organization's site strategy. Once the full location feasibility assessment is complete, the SWP practitioner should shift focus to providing input to the organization's facilities design team on the development of an optimal space in which employees can work. In recent years, increasingly more organizations have turned to more customized and elaborate workplace designs, in the hope of increasing productivity, collaboration and creativity. As in the site-selection process, the SWP practitioner can provide valuable research and insight into how a workspace should be designed to provide maximum utility for the targeted workforce. Factors to consider in this component of the analysis include:

- employee workplace expectations;
- workplace productivity;
- open versus closed concept;
- comfort;
- meeting rooms;
- workspace amenities and perks;
- workspace technology.

Conclusion

This chapter has discussed the many reasons for organizations to think strategically about where they choose to locate their offices and operations. As has been discussed, often one of the strategic factors that organizations consider when choosing a location is that location's ability to attract and retain talent. This chapter has highlighted the fact that the SWP process can be a valuable tool in helping the organization to select and optimize a location to ensure it will attract, retain and grow the talent required to drive optimal company performance.

Strategic workforce planning for contractors and the contingent workforce

09

CHAPTER OBJECTIVES

1 Define the role of contingent workers and contractors as part of the broader workforce.

2 Weigh up the costs and benefits of the contingent and contractor workforce strategy.

3 Outline a framework for incorporating contingent workers and contractors into the Strategic Workforce Plan.

4 Outline a framework for choosing a master service provider (MSP) and vendor management system (VMS).

Understanding contingent workers and contractors as part of the workforce

Contingent workers and contractors are the employees of an organization that are not considered to be official FTEs. These workers typically work for the company under some form of contract for a fixed amount of time (Allan, 2002). Depending on their performance, the projects they are working on and the value they are providing to the company, their contracts may or may not be renewed when their obligation ends. The biggest difference between contingent workers, contractors and FTEs involves the duration of work they do for the company, the types of benefits they receive and the method by which the workers' taxes are paid (the tax methodology can vary by country). While contingent workers and contractors at first may appear to be the same thing, there are slight nuances in the differences between the two that should be clearly understood.

Contingent workers

Thinking of a contingent worker as a 'freelancer' who provides their skills to companies in the form of services is a simple way to distinguish the work they do from that of a regular FTE. Contingent workers are more flexible than contractors in the way in which they work and get paid. This form of worker may work under contract, perform ad hoc work on a temporary basis or work on projects for companies as a consultant. It is important to note that the organization should view contingent workers as fully autonomous in how they perform the work they do. What this means is that these workers truly work for themselves and as such have the ability to decide how they will scope, execute and deliver on the projects on which they work.

Contractors

Contractors, on the other hand, have less flexibility regarding how they will conduct the work they are undertaking. While the implications of being a contractor vary by country, in the United States, when employees fall under a 'contractual' commitment the organization has more flexibility regarding the termination of that contract. Obviously, this depends on the structure and terms of the original signed and agreed contract, but, generally speaking, if the worker is not meeting the expectations the company laid forth in that original contract, it has legal grounds to terminate that contract. From a tax standpoint, the organization may calculate tax for an employee under contract in a similar fashion to how it would if that employee was a regular FTE.

Utilizing contingent workers and contractors

So, why do companies use contingent workers and contractors and how do they factor into the organization's broader workforce strategy? There are various reasons why an organization might want to include contingent workers and contractors as part of its workforce strategy (see Figure 9.1). Perhaps the biggest reason is they provide the organization with an extra layer of flexibility to supplement short-term projects and skills gaps that the organization may be facing (Mallon and Duberley, 2000). Depending on the industry and specific day-to-day tasks involved in the company's operations, contingent workers and contractors can also help to increase productivity for the organization (Purcell, 1998). For businesses that face peaks and valleys in demand for their services or products, productivity gains through contingent workers and contractors can be especially useful. For example, a company that has a call centre to deal with customer service issues might face demand seasonality. Contingent workers can provide the organization with a buffer of flexibility and, at the same time, a low level of risk to meet this demand. More concerning using contractors and contingent workers for risk mitigation purposes will be discussed later in the chapter.

Including contingent workers and contractors as part of the broader workforce strategy also can alleviate some of the administrative burden associated with FTEs. The organization will not have to deal with performance evaluations, interviews and the cumbersome paperwork and documentation that is often required when dealing with FTEs. Reducing these administrative burdens allows the

Figure 9.1 Benefits of a contingent and contractor workforce strategy

Flexibility	Cost Savings	Less Administrative Burden	Talent Pool
Provides a layer of workforce flexibility for the ups and downs of the business cycle	Can provide significant cost savings from taxes and benefits administration	Less administrative in areas such as performance reviews etc compared to FTEs	Provides access to an entirely new talent pool

Contingent and Contractor Workforce

organization's FTEs to focus on more value-adding activities, which can add up to significant efficiency and productivity gains for the company over the long term.

Another major reason for enhancing the workforce with contingent workers and contractors is the potential cost savings they represent for the organization. As opposed to FTEs who are paid benefits, hourly wages and salaries no matter what their output, contingent workers and contractors are essentially only paid for what they are producing. Depending upon the country in which the organization operates, there is also the potential to save a significant amount of money on taxes. In the United States for example, organizations do not have to withhold social security and Medicare taxes for their contingent workforce, which can once again save the company large sums of money over the long run.

Contingent workers and contractors also introduce the organization to an entirely new 'talent pool' than they might otherwise have accessed. The reason for this is because organizations typically get many of their contingent workers through a master service provider (MSP; there will be an in-depth discussion on MSPs later in the chapter). These MSPs act as the intermediary between the contingent workers and the organizations that require these workers. Consequently, the MSPs are effectively providing their own mini talent pool for the organizations that use them.

In addition to providing access to a new supply of talent, many organizations view contingent workers and contractors as being potential FTEs in the future. Having these workers in a more temporary status as contractors or contingent workers provides managers with the opportunity to give these workers a trial run to see if they might be a good fit for an FTE role at some point in the future. It is no surprise that many managers feel more comfortable converting a contingent worker or contractor to an FTE role when they have had the opportunity to get to know them and their working style instead of hiring a candidate they know little about.

Trends in the contingent and contractor workforce

In order for the SWP practitioner to incorporate the contingent and contractor workforce as a broader component of the Strategic

Workforce Plan, it is important that they understand some of the current trends in the contingent or contractor workforce industry. Contingent workers and contractors are not a new phenomenon in the workforce. Companies have been using this form of worker for decades. What is new, however, is the volume and sheer number of companies that have started using them over the last several years. It is also important to note that the increased popularity of the contingent and contractor workforce is not limited to just the companies using them, but also comprises job seekers who actively look for this form of employment. Being a 'freelancer' has dramatically increased in popularity over the last several years as the freedom and flexibility that come from a career option of this nature continue to entice people from many different walks of life and professional backgrounds. A recent 2016 study by Paychex (an online HR services firm) revealed that, between 2000 and 2014, the freelance economy has grown by over 500 per cent (Paychex, 2016). This confluence of employers looking for contractors and contingent workers to supplement their workforce and potential candidates in the workforce seeking jobs to fulfil that demand has led to a monumental shift in the way work is performed around the world. There are even new terms to describe this form of work such as 'gig' or 'on-demand' economy. One need look no further than ride-hailing companies like Uber and Lyft to see how the gig economy has dramatically changed the way in which service is provided and work is performed around the world.

For the SWP practitioner, the key takeaway here is that the contingent workforce will continue to increase in popularity. What this means for the SWP practitioner is that factoring this facet of the workforce into the broader Strategic Workforce Plan will become increasingly more important as the on-demand workforce becomes a bigger component of the workforce for many companies. So, where to begin? As a starting point, the SWP practitioner should work with HR and business leaders to perform an analysis and develop a strategy that will address some of the following questions regarding the future of contractors and the contingent workforce:

- How will the trend of increasing the number of contingent workers and contractors as a percentage of the total labour supply affect the ability to source talent for FTE roles in the organization?

- How will the organization differentiate its talent brand to appeal to the labour force that is more interested in being part of the gig economy?

- As increasingly more of an organization's total workforce is made up of contingent workers and contractors, how will the organization deal with developing and managing talent across this new facet of the workforce?

Costs and benefits of the contingent and contractor workforce strategy

Like any strategic decision that an organization makes, some specific costs and benefits should be considered when deciding on a specific approach to the organization's contingent and contractor workforce strategy. Helping the organization to weigh up the costs and benefits of this decision is another opportunity for the SWP practitioner to provide insights and add value to the organization's broader workforce strategy. As shown in Figure 9.2, there are three key areas relating to an organization's contingent and contractor workforce

Figure 9.2   Contingent and contractor workforce insights provided by the SWP function

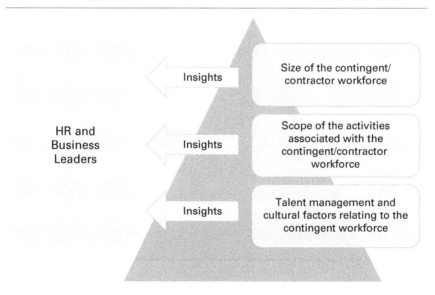

strategy about which the SWP practitioner should provide HR and business leaders with insights. These three areas are:

- size of the contingent and contractor workforce;
- scope of the activities and work the contingent and contractor workforce will undertake in the organization;
- talent management and cultural factors relating to how the organization's FTEs and contingent workers and contractors interact and work together on a day-to-day basis.

Size of the contingent workforce

The first question the company needs to grapple with regarding the contingent and contractor workforce strategy is: how much of the organization's total workforce should be made up of contingent workers and contractors? Answering this question is important because the relative size of the contingent workforce potentially could have a significant impact on the culture of the organization. That said, if the cost savings and efficiency gains increase dramatically with every incremental addition to the contingent and contractor workforce, the organization might want to accept the risk of a diluted FTE base and culture in favour of the upside benefits to the bottom line. In this component of the analysis, the SWP practitioner should rank and weight the costs versus the benefits of increasing the proportion of contingent workers and contractors to FTEs. Potential benefits of this strategy include:

- tax savings (dependent upon the country);
- reduction in administrative tasks associated with hiring, onboarding and the exit process;
- access to additional pools of talent;
- more flexible workforce;
- ability to smooth cyclical or seasonal demand.

Possible costs and risks related to broadening the size of the contingent workforce include (Mallon and Duberley, 2000):

- legal and compliance risks (dependent upon the country);
- different management approach and style required;

- impact on the organization's culture;
- risk of internal leaks of sensitive company information.

A useful methodology for the SWP practitioner to use to weigh the costs versus the benefits of a larger contingent contractor workforce is to assign weights based on the importance of each factor to the organization. Once the organization has weighted each of the factors, subjective probabilities should then be assigned to each of these factors based on the likelihood of them occurring given the decision has been made to increase the proportion of contingent workers and contractors to FTEs. To fully benefit from this activity, the SWP practitioner should work with HR and business leaders to develop multiple scenarios that describe how the likelihood of each event occurring increases or decreases as the size of the contingent and contractor workforce grows or shrinks. Taking this approach will help to provide the organization with insights into the implications of the risk versus reward from different contingent and contractor worker to FTE ratios.

After the SWP practitioner has worked with the organization's leaders to assign weights and probabilities to each of the above factors, they should then multiply each weight by its accompanying probability for each scenario. Performing this basic calculation will reveal a set of scores to which the SWP practitioner can compare each scenario. Any scenario where the score for the costs and risks is greater than the benefits should be thrown out as an option. If all of the scenarios end up having benefits greater than the costs and risks, the scenario with the highest benefits score should be considered the most attractive ratio from a contingent worker/contractor to FTE standpoint. This information should be a starting point for making decisions concerning the size of the contingent and contractor workforce that the organization will pursue as part of its broader workforce strategy.

Incorporating contingent workers and contractors into the Strategic Workforce Plan

Developing a truly holistic Strategic Workforce Plan and accompanying workforce strategy involves combining all aspects of the workforce into that plan and strategy. Including contractors and the contingent workforce in that plan is something that the SWP practitioner should consider critical. As has been discussed throughout this book, the fundamental tenets involved in creating a basic Strategic Workforce Plan include:

1 understanding the corporate strategy and business drivers that impact on the workforce;

2 understanding the critical workforce segments across the organization;

3 analysing the current internal and external supply of skills and talent that make up the workforce.

Then, taking it one step further and developing projections for that supply and what the organization's requirements for those skills and talent should be in the future – all based on the organization's business drivers:

4 analysing the current demand for internal and external skills across the organization. Then, similarly to step 3, developing projections of what demand for those skills and talent should be in the future – once again based on the organization's business drivers;

5 developing strategies to address any gaps in skills and talent that the supply and demand analyses might have revealed.

Incorporating the contingent workforce and contractors into the organization's workforce strategy and finalized Strategic Workforce Plan involves taking the methodology and steps outlined above and layering in the contingent and contractor workforce into that plan (see Figure 9.3). Effectively, the SWP practitioner should treat the contingent workers and contractors as another element of the workforce that needs to be analysed and accounted for in the same way as FTEs.

The primary difference between the approach the SWP practitioner takes for developing the contingent worker/contractor and FTE portions of the Strategic Workforce Plan has to do with the type of questions that SWP practitioner asks. The following section will review example questions that should be asked in the context of the contingent and contractor workforce for each of the key areas of the Strategic Workforce Plan.

Figure 9.3 SWP for the contingent and contractor workforce

Corporate strategy and business drivers

- Is the corporate strategy placing a greater emphasis on cost controls moving into the future? If so, is moving to a larger ratio of contractors and contingent workers an option for reducing costs?

- Is the company in an industry like oil and gas where significant swings in macroeconomic factors such as oil prices can lead to massive cost-cutting and downsizing to weather these business cycles? If so, could contractors and contingent workers provide more flexibility to the organization when downturns require reductions in the workforce?

- Does the organization have plans for some portion of the business model to become 'on demand' like Uber or Airbnb? If so, will this require building a contingent workforce to meet these new workforce requirements?

Critical workforce segments

- Do contingent workers and contractors make up their own workforce segment or are they allocated across the workforce segments identified for FTEs?

- Do the requirements for contractors and contingent workers remain steady across all sites, countries and regions, or do they vary depending upon those sites, countries or regions?

- Looking across the contractor and contingent workforce, are there certain roles in this workforce that drive a disproportionate amount of value? If so, should the organization consider converting these roles into FTE roles?

- For the contractor and contingent segments that have been identified as critical, how is the organization working with the MSP to ensure there is a healthy pipeline of talent from which to source candidates?

Talent supply and demand

- Does the future of the corporate strategy require skill sets that are in limited supply? If so, can the supply of these skills be met through the contingent workers and contractors?

- Are there future skills and jobs that the organization will not be able to source as FTEs? Can the organization source these skills from contractors or contingent workers instead?

- Are there any jobs or skill sets found in the gig economy that are increasing in demand in the external market? Will this impact on the organization's ability to source these jobs or skills in the future?

- Will the increase in demand for contractors and contingent workers that possess certain skill sets grow at the same rate as the demand for FTEs with similar skill sets?

- Are there pockets of contingent workers and contractors with critical talent in certain regions or areas of the world or is this critical talent dispersed around the globe in a more even fashion?

Developing strategies to address talent gaps

- Were there talent gaps discovered in the FTE gap analysis? If so, is there an opportunity to reduce that gap with contingent workers or contractors?

- Should the organization be investing more money in training and developing FTEs or rather invest that money in building out a larger workforce of contingent workers and contractors?

- Should the organization focus on hiring and retaining unproven FTEs or develop a strategy of converting high-performing contractors or contingent workers into FTEs instead?

Incorporating the contingent worker and contractor component of the workforce into the broader Strategic Workforce Plan is not as complicated as it may seem. Doing so mostly entails going through the same steps that the organization went through in developing the plan for FTEs but looking through the lens of contingent workers and contractors. The biggest challenge the SWP practitioner will face is thinking through the nuances regarding the questions that should be asked when assessing the current and future state of the contingent and contractor workforce. If they have already gone through the activity with the FTEs, however, when the time comes to do the same for the contingent workers and contractors, the exercise will be likely to feel less complicated.

Choosing a master service provider and vendor management system

Perhaps one of the most important factors to consider in building a strong contingent and contractor workforce strategy is selecting a good MSP and vendor management system (VMS) with which to work. As it relates to an organization's contingent and contractor workforce strategy, an MSP is essentially a third-party vendor that the organization works with to help manage the company's contingent workers, contractors and associated staffing agencies. A typical MSP works at the client's site (although this is not always the case) and may be one individual or part of a small team. MSPs tend to be large companies that deploy smaller teams to work with or at their clients' sites. The primary role of MSPs as part of the organization's broader contingent worker and contractor strategy is to help the organization manage the day-to-day administrative aspect of working with staffing agencies to find suitable contractors and contingent workers. MSPs directly support the company in onboarding candidates, gathering feedback on the performance of the contractors and contingent workers performing activities and ensuring the organizations' needs are being met by the staffing agencies providing those candidates. On a side note, MSP is also used as an acronym to describe similar types of service providers outside of the contingent workforce and contractor industry. For example, organizations often have MSPs for their supply chain operations that are entirely separate entities from the MSPs discussed in this chapter.

A VMS, on the other hand, is merely a technology solution to help manage more of the administrative aspects of the contingency and contractor strategy. Organizations typically use a VMS as a method for relaying candidate hiring requirements, inputting job requisitions, selecting candidates, providing feedback on the quality of work that the contractors and contingent workers are performing and, finally, handling the actual third-party transactions along with supporting the billing and payment process.

Because MSPs and VMSs have the potential to be such a significant component of the organization's contingent and contractor workforce strategy, it is crucial that an organization selects vendors that will make good partners to work with on the organization's contingent and contractor workforce strategy. In addition to being a partner on this strategy, these vendors should also help to reduce some of the risks that contingent workers and contractors can introduce to the organization's broader workforce strategy as outlined earlier in the chapter.

Since MSPs and VMSs stand to have such a tremendous impact on the organization's chances of successfully executing on its contingent worker and contractor strategy, it is imperative to select vendors that will help and not hinder the company's ability to do this. The SWP practitioner should work directly with HR and business leaders to develop criteria and an assessment methodology for choosing vendors with which to work. The following section will provide an overview of important criteria to include in the vendor selection process and will discuss a methodology against which the organization can compare these vendors.

Criteria to include in the MSP and VMS assessment process

Key criteria against which the SWP practitioner can compare the MSP and VMS include the following:

- customer service;
- MSP/VMS systems integration;
- risk and compliance;
- analytics;
- vendor spend;
- talent management;
- technology usability;
- ability to provide references.

Customer service

When it comes to the relationship between the vendor and the organization using the vendor's services, a true partnership should exist. What that means is a vendor should be in place that is responsive and provides excellent customer service. If the organization is going to invest a significant amount of money on an MSP or VMS solution, it should expect the provider to understand the company, listen to the company's concerns and be willing to be flexible to allow for the dynamic nature in which most organizations operate.

MSP/VMS systems integration

As discussed earlier, MSPs and VMSs are separate services that can help organizations manage their contingent and contractor workforces. That said, MSPs and VMSs both offer unique qualities to help manage that component of the workforce. In an optimal scenario, the organization would find MSPs and VMSs that have an ability to integrate with each other. Even more ideal would be to find a vendor that offers both an MSP and a VMS component in their service offering. Finding a provider that offers both of these services will create a more holistic platform that will reduce the amount of complexity in the final service offering. Additionally, and more specifically with respect to the VMS, it is a desirable attribute if the VMS provider possesses a flexible enough platform to integrate with some of the organization's broader technology systems.

Risk and compliance

In recent years many organizations have started to use contractors and contingent workers not only as a method to supplement talent, but also as a tactic to reduce the amount of taxes they have to pay. For companies to realize these tax savings legally, however, the specifications for roles that contingent workers or contractors occupy have to comply with specific government regulations (in the United States). If companies do not comply with these regulations, they can face hefty fines. It is important, then, for the organization to work with an MSP or VMS provider whose service offering will reduce the exposure to risk associated with these regulations.

Analytics

As organizations move increasingly more towards data insights to drive decision making, the importance of choosing an MSP or VMS provider that provides the company with the ability to analyse and track the performance of the contingent and contractor workforce is essential. Regarding the broader Strategic Workforce Plan, as the SWP practitioner begins to merge contractors and the contingent workforce into the FTE workforce strategy, having access to these insights will be a valuable tool when making strategic decisions to optimize this component of the workforce.

Vendor spend

It goes without saying that, if the organization has partnered with a particular MSP or VMS provider and that vendor is spending money on the organization's behalf to source candidates and in turn passing those costs on to the organization, that organization will want insight into the details of where the vendor is spending its money. It is important to ensure the final MSP provider the organization chooses to partner with provides insight and visibility concerning where the organization's money is being spent.

Talent management

Most organizations develop internal cultures that shape how strategic objectives are accomplished and how the day-to-day work is completed. Maintaining this organizational culture requires systems and processes that are in place to manage talent. It is important that the organization partners with an MSP and VMS provider that can ensure the candidates they are providing will not be disruptive to the current corporate culture in place. To do this requires that the vendor has thought through and can articulate how they will manage the talent they are providing. It is imperative that, before choosing a final vendor to partner with, there is a clear understanding concerning how that vendor will ensure the contingent worker and contractor talent will be managed appropriately.

Technology usability

Another consideration, more specifically relating to the VMS, is the usability of the technology. If the software is such that it is too complicated for the end user to figure out, much of the value that is supposed to be derived from it will be lost. To that end, it is important to assess the software's user interface for usability. Ultimately, the vendor should provide a technology that drives adoption across the organization. A clunky or difficult-to-use tool can be intimidating for end users and ultimately end up being more of a hindrance than a valuable option for the organization looking to use it.

Ability to provide references

The final aspect to include in the assessment criteria for making an MSP or VMS decision is references or customer reviews. Having the vendor provide the organization with references is a crucial aspect to understanding the strengths and weaknesses of the product or service. Customer references are so important that it makes sense to try and get them from both the vendor and independent third-party sources. Taking a two-pronged approach will ensure that the reviews received are not biased in the direction of the vendor.

Determining the best choice of vendor

Once the criteria have been established, the SWP practitioner should once again ensure a methodology is in place against which to compare multiple vendors. A simple but efficient method to apply for this assessment is to weight each factor by the importance level it represents for the organization. From there, each variable should be ranked across each vendor that was assessed using a score of 1–10 (with 10 being the best). Next, each variable should be multiplied by the weight assigned to it according to the rank it was given against the other vendors. Once these multipliers have been applied to each variable, the scores should be added up. The vendor with the highest score should be considered the optimal choice for the organization to pursue as its contingent worker and contractor workforce partner.

Summary of chapter objectives

The role of contingent workers and contractors as part of the broader workforce

There are various reasons why an organization might want to include contingent workers and contractors as part of its work-force strategy. Some of the top reasons organizations look to include contingent workers and contractors as part of their broader workforce include:

- tax savings (dependent upon the country);
- reduction in administrative tasks associated with hiring, onboarding and the exit process;
- access to additional pools of talent;
- more flexible workforce;
- ability to smooth cyclical or seasonal demand.

The costs and benefits of a contingent and contractor workforce strategy

Like any strategic decision an organization makes, some specific costs and benefits should be considered when deciding on a specific approach to the organization's contingent and contractor workforce strategy. Helping the organization weigh up the costs and benefits of this decision is another opportunity for the SWP practitioner to provide insights and add value to the organization's broader workforce strategy. There are three key areas relating to an organization's contingent and contractor workforce strategy about which the SWP practitioner should provide HR and business leaders with insights. These three areas are:

- size of the contingent and contractor workforce;
- scope of the activities and work the contingent workforce will do in the organization;
- talent management and cultural factors relating to how the organization's FTEs and those contingent workers and contractors interact and work together on a day-to-day basis.

Incorporating contingent workers and contractors into the Strategic Workforce Plan

Developing a truly holistic Strategic Workforce Plan and accompanying workforce strategy involves combining all aspects of the workforce into that plan and strategy. Including contractors and the contingent workforce in that plan is something that the SWP practitioner should consider to be critical. The process of incorporating contingent workers and contractors into the Strategic Workforce Plan is almost identical to the process involved for regular FTEs. The primary difference between the approach the SWP practitioner takes for developing the contingent worker and FTE portions of the Strategic Workforce Plan has to do with the type of questions that SWP practitioner asks.

Choosing an MSP and a VMS

Perhaps one of the biggest factors to consider in building out a strong contingent and contractor workforce strategy is selecting a good MSP and VMS with which to work. Key criteria against which the SWP practitioner can compare the MSP and VMS include the following:

- customer service;
- MSP/VMS systems integration;
- risk and compliance;
- analytics;
- vendor spend;
- talent management;
- technology usability;
- ability to provide references.

Conclusion

As the gig or freelance economy continues to grow in popularity and become an ever-increasing method of employment for both employees and employers, it becomes increasingly more important for the SWP process to ensure that this aspect of the workforce is accounted for in the broader Strategic Workforce Plan. Furthermore, the importance of including contractors and contingent workers in the workforce strategy will only increase in the coming years as the popularity of this form of work gains exponential momentum and will begin to account for increasingly larger proportions of the workforce for many organizations.

Workforce analytics

10

CHAPTER OBJECTIVES

1 Define workforce analytics.

2 Outline when workforce analytics should be used.

3 Outline the workforce analytics maturity curve.

4 Define the role of workforce analytics in SWP.

Workforce analytics

Workforce analytics – sometimes called people analytics or HR analytics – fundamentally is a data-driven approach to gaining insight into factors that have the potential to impact on an organization's workforce (Carlson and Kavanagh, 2011). Through data visualization and analysis, metrics, dashboards and statistics, workforce analytics seeks to answer three key questions (see Figure 10.1) regarding workforce-related events that take place in an organization (eg attrition or promotions):

- Why did it happen?
- Why is it happening?
- When will it happen next?

Workforce analytics is not a new phenomenon, but it is one that has become significantly more popular in recent years (Carlson and Kavanagh, 2011). Several factors have contributed to this increased interest in workforce analytics. In the era of big data, many

Figure 10.1   Three key questions that workforce analytics seeks to answer

organizations have been forced to develop data and analytics strategies in order to remain competitive in their chosen industries. Not having a data and analytics strategy or vision in place can be catastrophic for organizations trying to compete in ever-more competitive markets. Companies that do not develop data and analytics strategies risk watching their competitors gain an advantage on them by adopting strategies that do leverage the available data. It is for this reason that most companies, willing or not, have been forced to become more data driven. For a large number of these organizations, however, this data-driven approach to conducting business was not something that was always in the scope of their HR functions. That changed, however, as time passed and astute organizations like Google began to realize that the vast stores of 'people' data available to them created opportunities to take the same data-driven approach to the workforce that was being applied to the rest of the business. Soon, leveraging data and analytics to improve decision making became more mainstream, which led to many companies starting to look to the HR function to become as data driven as the rest of the organization. It was when this started happening that workforce analytics gained momentum and began to become the new standard in HR.

Another factor that led to an uprising in the popularity of workforce analytics was the advancement in HR technology and systems (Carlson and Kavanagh, 2011). As the popularity of workforce analytics began to increase, large HRIS database and warehousing companies began expanding their offerings to include some basic dashboarding and analytics capabilities in their products. At the same time, smaller software companies started to pop up that provided more user-friendly dashboards and analytics products. These workforce analytics software solutions were especially attractive to HR practitioners who may not have been as comfortable with data and analytics as employees in other functions who used data and analytics more often in their day-to-day activities.

Media exposure is another reason why there has been an uprising in the popularity of workforce analytics. There have been some high-profile stories written about the success Google and similar companies have had with workforce analytics that have led to additional buzz in the HR community. HR-focused magazines and related websites also have been writing stories on the power of workforce analytics. In addition to these regular media outlets writing stories on the topic, it is also something that has become popular for bloggers to write about and is a frequent topic at HR conferences on the conference circuit. In fact, the popularity of workforce analytics has gained so much steam that there are many conferences around the world solely dedicated to the topic.

When should workforce analytics be used?

Regarding the usefulness of workforce analytics and when it should be used, a better question might be to ask: when should workforce analytics not be used? A key concept in management is the idea of providing managers with the autonomy to make decisions that will be in the best interests of their respective organizations. These organizations are essentially expecting their managers to make decisions that will lead to positive business outcomes and 'add value' to their company's bottom line. That said, it is not enough to expect these managers to just blindly make decisions that will benefit the organization. Rather, there should be an expectation that these managers use a combination of their experience, intuition and ability while, most importantly, also relying on data to make truly optimal decisions. Typically, this level of data-driven decision making is associated with finance, marketing or operational decisions. For an organization to think that data-driven decision making should only apply to these functions is a big mistake. In fact, given how much of the total expenses of an organization's budget is usually accounted for by the workforce, the argument probably can be made that workforce analytics and the use of data-driven decision making in HR is even more important than the functions outlined above. With this in mind, workforce analytics can be a useful tool for organizations and managers to use to provide insight into the workforce which can lead to enhanced decision making for improved workforce performance and ultimately a competitive advantage (Davenport, Harris and Shapiro, 2010).

The statement that workforce analytics should be applied any time a decision is made regarding the workforce in and of itself might not be particularly useful to the SWP practitioner who might be looking for more practical and actionable ideas regarding where and when to apply workforce analytics. That said, this section will cover more specific areas where applying workforce analytics to make better workforce-related decisions can be more helpful to the SWP practitioner in the context of optimal SWP (see Figure 10.2).

Recruiting talent

For many companies, the ability to attract top candidates with the right skills at the right time is so important that it becomes a pillar of not only their talent strategy but also their corporate strategy. Organizations that fall into this category use talent as a tool for gaining a competitive advantage in the industries in which they compete. For companies that do compete on talent, the ability to have clear insight into what is or is not working in their recruiting pipeline

Figure 10.2 Workforce analytics should be used to improve decision making regarding the organization's workforce

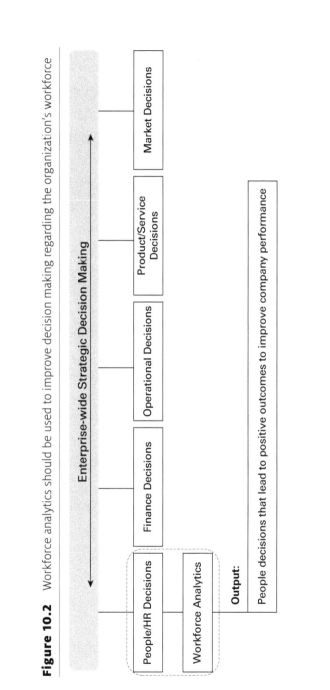

Enterprise-wide Strategic Decision Making

People/HR Decisions

Finance Decisions

Operational Decisions

Product/Service Decisions

Market Decisions

Workforce Analytics

Output:

People decisions that lead to positive outcomes to improve company performance becomes especially important. More specifically, these organizations can use workforce analytics to better understand things such as:

- The effectiveness of the recruiting process. On average, how much is the company spending to recruit top talent?
- On average, how long does it take to recruit this top talent?
- Where should the organization search to find this top talent?
- Are there any trends in the external talent market that could impact on the organization's future talent strategy?
- What competitors possess candidates that might be more likely to leave their current companies in favour of a new company?
- What benefits and perks should the organization highlight in its employer brand proposition to attract potential candidates when reaching out to them for the first time?
- What candidate profiles are more likely to make it through the interview process?
- What candidate profiles are more likely not only to make it through the recruitment process but also to be productive and successful employees once they are working for the company?
- Based on candidate profiles, are there differences in the types of candidates that might be more likely to fall out of the recruitment process? If so, why?
- How can the organization develop interviews and an assessment process that are optimized for accuracy in predicting which candidates will be successful based on their performance in interviews?
- How can the organization develop interview training material that improves the key attributes required to assess a candidate's skills and behavioural traits accurately?

Retaining talent

For organizations that are competing on talent – and for those that are not for that matter – recruiting this top talent is not always enough. Organizations must also be able to retain this top talent.

There are various reasons why companies develop retention strategies, but a few of the most salient reasons are:

- The cost of recruiting new hires to fill the roles of the employee who left is expensive.

- Every time an employee leaves the company, they take with them the intellectual capital they gained while working for that company. Intellectual capital is invaluable to organizations and, once it is gone, it will take time to replace. The impact of this effect is magnified by the length of time the employee was with the company.

- Every time a new employee is hired, it takes time for the organization to train and build their skills before they become fully productive. This same process has to be applied to employees who are being hired as backfill to replace employees who have left the company. The costs and productivity loss of training new hires due to backfill can be very high.

The reasons above highlight the high cost and detrimental impact of losing top talent for an organization. Workforce analytics can be a valuable tool for identifying factors that can lead to attrition. Specifically, workforce analytics can provide the organization's leaders with insights into some of the following topics relating to attrition:

- What are the top factors that drive attrition in the organization?

- Independent of the factors identified above, how much do compensation and benefits contribute to retaining top talent?

- Is attrition higher or lower for the organization's top talent and why?

- Are there pockets of the organization where attrition is too low (a certain amount of attrition is a good thing, preventing the organization from beginning to stagnate in terms of creativity and fresh thinking)? If so, why?

- Does attrition vary by demographics across the organization – eg millennials versus baby-boomers? If so, why?

- Are there differences in attrition by location and site? If so, why?

- Are there differences in attrition between salaried and hourly employees? If so, why?

- Are there certain roles and skill sets that are more likely to see higher attrition rates? If so, why?

- Is attrition trending up or down across all the organizational dimensions mentioned above? If so, why?

- How much do external macroeconomic forces impact on the organization's attrition rates?

- What is the actual cost of attrition? Are these costs growing or shrinking? If so, why?

- Based on where the organization is in its business cycle, is attrition even a problem? For example, is the company in a restructuring or downsizing mode?

- Is the importance of retaining top talent relatively stable or will it become more important in the future due to external factors like skills shortages in the external talent market?

Developing talent

If the organization is focusing on attracting and retaining top talent, it goes without saying that it will be likely to want to develop that talent as well. Depending on the organization's philosophy regarding talent development, there are a variety of different approaches that could be pursued to accomplish this. In a similar way to retaining and attracting talent, workforce analytics can provide significant insight into informing decisions regarding the best approach to take for the development of this talent. Questions that can be answered with workforce analytics on this topic include:

- Does the organization's current approach to developing talent impact on performance? If so, is it a positive or negative impact and why?

- Are there certain training programmes that are more effective than others? If so, why?

- What is the right amount of training to provide for employees given the cost and benefits that the training provides?

- Should all employees receive the same level of training or should training requirements be a function of the employee's job and that job's criticality to the organization?

- Are there differences in the effectiveness of training if the training is mandatory versus voluntary? If so, why?

- Is there a particular method for delivering training that is more effective than others? If so, why?

- What are the variables or characteristics that make one training programme more effective than another?

- Are there particular demographics or pockets of talent within the organization that respond better or worse to training programmes? If so, why?

- Does the effectiveness of training vary by site or location? If so, why?

- For global organizations, do cultural factors impact on the effectiveness of the training? If so, why?

- Are there any trends in the effectiveness of the organization's current approach to training? Is the training becoming more or less effective? If so, why?

- Are there differences in the effectiveness of on-the-job training versus classroom or virtual training? If so, why and how large is the difference?

- What is the cost of delivering the training versus the impact that training is having on productivity?

- Has the cost of training been increasing or decreasing? If so, why?

Performance management

Understanding the drivers of employee performance is essential for organizations if there is an expectation that managers will use a performance management system to improve employee performance. Workforce analytics is one of the best tools managers can use to understand the conditions that lead to one employee performing better or worse than another. If done correctly, workforce analytics can help to answer some of the following questions related to managing employee performance:

- All things being equal, are there environmental factors that contribute to one employee performing better or worse than another employee? If so, what are those factors?

- All things being equal, are there factors in the workforce such as age or tenure that lead to higher or lower performance? If so, why?

- Are there certain pools in the workforce that perform better or worse than others? If so, why?

- Are there employees with particular backgrounds, education or experience levels that contribute to better or worse performance than other employees? If so, what are these?

- Are there certain sites or locations where performance is better or worse than at other sites or locations? If so, why?

- When it comes to giving employees performance ratings, is the performance management system objective or is there bias in the system? If there is bias in the system, how prevalent is that bias and why?

- Are managers with a particular profile more or less likely to give better or worse performance ratings? If so, how do those manager profiles look?

- Do the organization's performance ratings fall under a normal distribution? Is this distribution forced or natural?

- Are the performance attributes that are being evaluated related to the behaviours that lead to improved organizational performance?

- Are there any discernible trends regarding performance ratings? Are performance ratings on average remaining static, increasing or decreasing? If so, why?

- Are there pockets of talent in the organization where performance ratings are improving or getting worse? If so, why?

Employee engagement and satisfaction

Many organizations conduct annual or biannual surveys to get a sense of how engaged and satisfied employees are in their jobs and with the company as a whole. It is not surprising that the best way to assess the results of these surveys is through workforce analytics. If done correctly and with more advanced statistical methods, workforce analytics can eradicate the random noise from the survey results and provide managers and organizational leaders with clear insights regarding the factors that drive engagement and satisfaction in the workforce. Workforce engagement and satisfaction questions that can be answered through workforce analytics include questions such as:

- What are the primary drivers of employee engagement and satisfaction? Are these drivers based on factors that the organization is in control of or are there outside factors that have an impact on engagement and satisfaction levels?

- Do demographic factors like tenure impact on job satisfaction? If so, why?

- Are there certain jobs or skill sets that are more or less likely to be engaged and satisfied than others? If so, why?

- Does engagement and job satisfaction vary by location? If so, why?

- Does culture play a role in job satisfaction? If so, what are the cultural factors that are leading to higher or lower job satisfaction levels?

- Assuming that questions concerning compensation are in the scope of the survey, do the compensation and benefits the organization offers contribute to higher or lower job satisfaction levels?

- Are there any relationships between engagement, satisfaction and higher or lower attrition rates? If so, why?

- Does manager approval impact on engagement and job satisfaction?

- Does company performance impact on engagement and job satisfaction? If so, why?

- Do factors like commute time and work-life balance impact on engagement and job satisfaction?

- Are there any trends in engagement and job satisfaction? Are the trends positive or negative and, if so, why?

The preceding examples are only the tip of the iceberg regarding the topics and questions that workforce analytics can help

Figure 10.3 Workforce analytics can be applied across a variety of HR and talent management activities

the organization gain insights into (see Figure 10.3). Although it is outside the scope of this book, it is also important to note that answering many of these questions requires the organization to have a few fundamental components in place regarding data and statistical skill sets. Performing many of the above analyses requires a certain degree of statistical aptitude and data quantity and quality. There will be more on this in future chapters, but suffice to say that conducting some of these analyses can be very complicated.

Workforce analytics maturity curve

The previous section touched briefly on the fact that the organization needs certain statistical skills and clean data to be able to conduct some of the more sophisticated analysis associated with gaining insight into many of the aspects of talent management discussed thus far. This section will provide an introduction to the workforce analytics maturity curve. The workforce analytics maturity curve essentially outlines the level of insight and types of question the organization realistically can expect to answer based on the systems, processes and skills that are in place for that organization's workforce analytics function. There are various versions of the workforce analytics maturity curve. Sometimes the curve is illustrated in the form of a pyramid, other times it is drawn out as a real curve. Regardless of the illustration's shape, there are four distinct classifications that workforce analytics functions typically fall into as they strive to provide deeper and more sophisticated insights on people-related issues.

Basic reporting

Basic reporting is the foundational phase of the workforce analytics maturity curve. In this phase, organizations typically are compiling basic reports from an HRIS data warehouse. The structure of these reports is generally raw data in the form of an Excel spreadsheet. The use case for reports of this nature typically involves the desire to gain insight into some very fundamental aspects of the workforce, like basic headcount by location, organization leader or function. The employee or contractor who creates the reports is usually an HRIS analyst who works directly in the HR function. That said, these duties also can be performed by analysts in other functions, assuming they have the necessary skill sets and access to the data. The minimum skill sets that the analyst requires at this stage are proficiency with structured query language (SQL) and basic Excel skills.

Dashboarding and metrics reporting

The next stage of the workforce analytics maturity curve is dashboarding and metrics reporting. This stage can be characterized by the creation of pivot tables, dashboards and more robust reporting. At this stage of the maturity curve, the objective goes from simply compiling basic reports to transforming and manipulating the data and content into charts, tables and visualizations that provide more intuitive insight into different dimensions of the workforce. Data no longer come from a single table in an HRIS system, but rather from multiple tables that are merged to create more customized reports and dashboards. It is at this stage of the workforce analytics maturity curve that organizations often begin to think through and establish basic metrics to track and measure the health of the organization's workforce. To that end, there is often more emphasis placed on analysing historical data to track and review changes in trends over time.

The skill-set requirements at this stage are similar to the first stage with the main difference being the depth of SQL expertise the analyst should possess to manipulate and merge the disparate data tables. It is also useful for the analyst to have experience with data visualization and dashboarding tools such as Tableau and advanced Excel charting. Because this stage also involves developing and creating metrics to include in the dashboards, it is a bonus if the analyst has a strong understanding of the business, operating model and key people challenges that the organization faces. In short, it is important for the analyst to possess strong business acumen to be optimally effective at this stage.

Descriptive insights

Descriptive insights are found at the next stage on the workforce analytics maturity curve. It is worth noting that the jump from dashboarding and metrics reporting to descriptive insights is relatively significant. The reason for this has to do with the skill sets that the organization will require at this stage. As opposed to the first two stages of the maturity curve that dealt with creating basic reports and dashboards from HRIS systems data, the descriptive insights stage is more focused on analysing the underlying data. At this stage, the organization begins to place greater emphasis on determining and analysing the root cause of and factors that may be contributing to workforce-related events or trends that are impacting the business. For example, in the descriptive insights stage, the organization might do a deep dive into the factors – hypothetically speaking – that might have led to a spike in attrition for a particular segment of the workforce. It is also worth mentioning that this is the first stage in which advanced statistical techniques are used in the analysis. At this stage, it is no longer enough to just create charts and visualize data; the analyst needs to distinguish and quantify random noise from statistically significant events that may appear in the data. They should be able to conduct a robust exploratory data analysis (EDA), and they should be able to test null and alternative hypotheses along with understanding how to assess the magnitude of statistically significant effects in the data.

Not surprisingly, the skill requirements for the analyst at this stage of the maturity curve shift from merely being proficient in SQL, Excel and data visualization to having deep domain expertise in statistics along with experience in programming languages like R and Python. A good analyst at this stage also should have a sense of curiosity regarding the data, understand the business issues facing the organization and have the communication skills to be able to simplify and articulate the results of a complicated statistical analysis to an audience that may not possess a background in statistics.

Predictive insights

The final stage of the workforce analytics maturity curve jumps from descriptive analytics, where the analyst is using statistical techniques to try and understand why a workforce-related event happened, to prescriptive analytics where the analyst is now attempting to predict what will occur in the future. Regarding the potential value that workforce analytics can provide to a company, this is the stage where that value can really start to be realized. If the organization gets to a point where it is no longer performing retrospective analyses on why something happened, but rather is performing proactive analyses to predict what will happen next, the organization's leaders can start taking measures to reduce the risks of detrimental workforce-related events occurring.

The skill sets required for this stage are primarily a combination of the skills needed for all the other stages with the addition of even more advanced statistical skills like machine learning and natural language processing. The sophistication level of the computer programming that the organization will require at this stage is also higher.

The role of workforce analytics in SWP

Until now, the focus of this chapter has been on understanding what workforce analytics is and how it can be used to gain more insight into workforce-related issues that could potentially impact on business performance. The discussion now will shift to drawing a link between workforce analytics and SWP. More specifically, answering the question of how the SWP practitioner can use workforce analytics to enhance the work they are doing on the organization's workforce strategy. The role of workforce analytics in SWP is so important that it would be nearly impossible to create a robust Strategic Workforce Plan without some form of input from workforce analytics. Workforce analytics is the aspect of SWP that helps the planning go from being an intuition-based activity to one that is quantified and grounded in facts. It allows the SWP practitioner to identify trends and issues in the workforce. Identifying these trends and issues is important in SWP because a large part of the final plan will be based on the actions required to mitigate against the risks identified by the workforce analytics. Workforce analytics is also the primary method the SWP practitioner uses to create forecasts and predictive models. Without workforce analytics, the SWP practitioner would not be able to develop quantified headcount forecasts or predictive attrition models. Being able to develop forecasts and predictive models of this nature is critical to the SWP practitioner if they are to develop plans to optimize the workforce's future performance. The following subsections provide details on specific components of SWP that either require or could benefit from workforce analytics (see Figure 10.4).

Attrition forecasting

For the SWP practitioner to create hiring forecasts that account for the full spectrum of hiring that the organization will require, they will need to build an attrition forecast to plan for backfills. A good attrition forecast should be grounded in statistics and falls clearly within the spectrum of workforce analytics.

Figure 10.4 Workforce analytics used in SWP activities

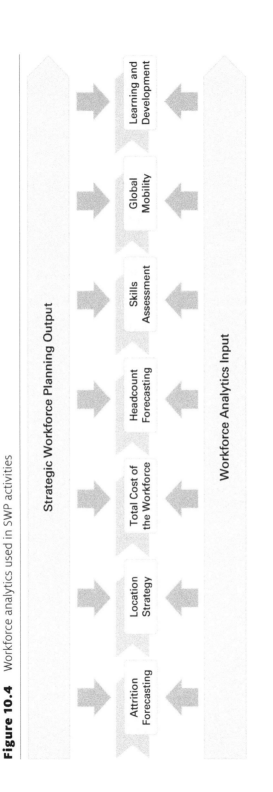

Strategic Workforce Planning Output

Attrition Forecasting | Location Strategy | Total Cost of the Workforce | Headcount Forecasting | Skills Assessment | Global Mobility | Learning and Development

Workforce Analytics Input

Headcount forecasts

A good headcount forecast should include two key components. The first is a qualitative top-down and bottom-up approach and the second is a more quantified regression analysis that predicts headcount based on the primary business drivers. The second element of the two can only be accomplished through statistics or, in other words, workforce analytics.

Skills assessment

A good skills assessment should attempt to quantify the level of aptitude that the organization possesses across the organization's skills and jobs. The quantification of this skills assessment can be accomplished through workforce analytics.

Total cost of the workforce

Calculating the total cost of the workforce is an analysis that involves simple calculations but many variables. This is an important aspect of SWP that utilizes workforce analytics to derive those final conclusions.

Location-based SWP

There are various aspects of workforce analytics involved in location-based SWP. Anything from performing cost-benefit analysis on the different sites to developing, ranking and applying criticality multipliers to the site-selection criteria falls under the umbrella of workforce analytics.

Learning and development

To optimize the productivity of the future workforce, the SWP practitioner needs to provide HR and business leaders with insight into where and how much training money the organization should spend across different workforce segments. Understanding the impact of training can be gained using workforce analytics.

Global mobility

It is important for the SWP practitioner to account for internal movement across the organization in the final Strategic Workforce Plan. Understanding the impact of this internal movement on the satisfaction and productivity of the workforce – which ultimately can shape the organization's point of view regarding global mobility – can be achieved using workforce analytics.

Workforce analytics and SWP

The preceding examples are just the start regarding the areas in which workforce analytics can be used in SWP. Because workforce analytics is such a crucial aspect of SWP, some organizations do not even differentiate between the two. If the two are differentiated, there should be a clear understanding of the importance that each holds for the other if the goal is to provide truly robust workforce-related insights to organizational leaders.

Summary of chapter objectives

What is workforce analytics?

At the most fundamental level workforce analytics is the practice of using data visualization and manipulation, metrics, dashboards and statistics to gain more insight into an organization's workforce. More specifically, workforce analytics seeks to answer three key questions regarding workforce-related events that take place in an organization (eg attrition or promotions):

- Why did it happen?
- Why is it happening?
- When will it happen next?

When should workforce analytics be used?

Simply put, workforce analytics can be used anytime business and HR leaders need to gain more insight into their organization's workforces. Workforce analytics can be used to track trends in the workforce, measure the effectiveness of a workforce-related programme or develop predictions concerning such areas as attrition or performance. Workforce analytics is not limited to a specific team, group or function within an organization either; rather, it can be used across the full suite of HR activities and also can be used by non-HR leaders. Specific topics where workforce analytics can be especially useful include:

- recruiting talent;
- retaining talent;
- developing talent;
- performance management;
- employee engagement and satisfaction.

Workforce analytics maturity curve

The workforce analytics maturity curve refers to a curve that tracks the sophistication and maturity of the workforce analytics in an organization. It is important for HR and business leaders to understand the workforce analytics maturity curve because it can provide guidance concerning the potential output that can be expected at each level of the curve along with providing insight into the sorts of skills required at each level to gain the insights associated with that level. This basically means the further the organization progresses along the curve, the more sophisticated the skills that will be required:

- basic reporting;
- dashboarding and metrics reporting;
- descriptive analytics;
- predictive insights.

The role of workforce analytics in SWP

Workforce analytics is one of the most important components of SWP. It is essentially the 'glue' that holds the SWP process together. Without workforce analytics, it would be nearly impossible for the SWP process to provide any real value when developing a workforce strategy. This is primarily because SWP uses data and analytics to gain insight into workforce-related gaps that exist today or potentially will exist in the future. Workforce analytics are what takes the SWP process from being a subjective exercise in guesswork to one that is quantified and founded in facts.

Conclusion

This chapter has provided the reader with an introduction to workforce analytics, opportunities to take advantage of workforce analytics and the role workforce analytics plays in SWP. Workforce analytics is so important in the SWP process that it is safe to say that, any time the term SWP is used in this book, there is also either a direct or indirect reference to workforce analytics.

Creating an effective strategic workforce planning function

11

Building the foundation for an SWP function

Organizations typically develop SWP functions because of some gap that exists in their ability to develop and execute on a workforce strategy (Schweyer, 2010). It is not uncommon for these organizations to build an SWP function simply as a 'knee-jerk' reaction to a workforce-related event that might have negatively impacted on the organization. Unfortunately, because these decisions are often reactionary, there is usually not enough upfront time focused on thinking through the design and some of the foundational aspects that might be relevant to the success of that SWP function over the long term. The potential implications of not having a solid foundation in place for the organization's SWP function can be huge. Not having a solid infrastructure in place can lead to confusion in the organization concerning what purpose the SWP function serves, what the expectations are for the function and, ultimately, what success looks like for that function.

There also can be a negative impact on the structure and composition of the SWP team if there is not enough upfront thought put into the skills and competencies the team requires for success. In particular, this can be troubling because not having the proper mix of skills, leadership and experience on the team can significantly impact on that team's ability to deliver the right level of actionable insights.

The scalability of the SWP function is another consideration that the organization should think through at the initial stage of the function's creation. The potential implications of not establishing clear processes and systems concerning how the SWP function will interact with the rest of the organization can have a detrimental impact on the function's ability to scale, grow and build momentum across the company.

Technology and data requirements also should be a consideration during the initial design of the SWP function. If the organization does not think through how the function will use data and technology to create and deliver insights, once again there could be scaling challenges and/or issues with the data quality and integrity.

A better approach for the organization to take after the decision has been made to implement an SWP team would be to spend a significant amount of upfront time assessing what foundational aspects need to be in place at the start of the organization's journey into SWP. If the organization does this correctly, it will help to maximize the probability that the creation of the team will add the value to the organization that is intended. There are essentially four key foundational pillars the organization should consider in the design phase of an SWP team:

1 What is the vision for the SWP team?

2 Who needs to be on the SWP team and what skills do they require?

3 What are the systems and processes that need to be in place to scale the SWP team?

4 What are the technology and data requirements that need to be in place for the SWP team to deliver actionable insights?

The remainder of the chapter will explore each of these pillars (see Figure 11.1) in greater detail.

Figure 11.1   The foundational pillars of a high-functioning SWP team

Crafting a vision for the SWP function

Studies have shown that the creation of a corporate vision can lead to improved company performance (Sidhu, 2003). The creation of a vision is as important for the SWP function as it is for the company as a whole. In fact, the starting point for the design of an effective and efficient SWP function should be the creation of a vision. Vision creation is a critical aspect in the early stages of designing an SWP function. It sets the tone and direction for the actions and milestones that the organization needs to accomplish to deliver on the function's broader objectives. Lack of the creation of vision in the early stages can be detrimental to allowing the SWP team to live up to its full potential. Without that vision, it becomes difficult for the organization to know the specific details that it should address when putting the initial building blocks in place. For example, assume an organization's vision is to develop an SWP function that will provide forecasts and guidance to HR business leaders on the talent mix and workforce profile it will require over the next three to five years. Now, further assume that this vision was never clearly articulated in the original design of that SWP function. If the vision for what this function's success looks like was not part of the upfront design process, it becomes impossible for that initial design to include all of the specifications that will be required to realize that vision. In other words, the SWP function in this example is attempting to navigate its way to some end goal in the dark. Creating a vision for the success of an SWP function is not an activity that the organization should take lightly nor is it an activity that should be completed in haste. Developing a vision for the SWP function involves three key areas (see Figure 11.2):

1 thinking through how the SWP function will contribute to the success of the company's broader mission;

2 narrowing in on the focus of the vision;

3 socialization and validation of the vision.

Figure 11.2 There are three key areas that should be addressed in the creation of an SWP vision

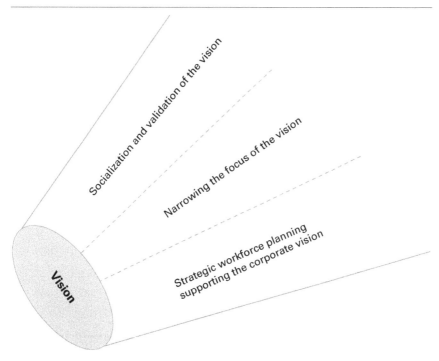

Aligning the SWP vision with the company's mission

A recurring theme throughout this book has been the importance of aligning the workforce strategy with the company's corporate strategy and vision. Developing a vision for the organization's SWP function is no different. What this means is that the first question organizational leaders should ask regarding the creation of that vision is: what is our corporate vision and how can the SWP function support the organization in its quest to achieve that vision? With the company's mission on the table as the backdrop for the discussion, organizational leaders should take this broad vision approach and begin to narrow in on the details of what the SWP function specifically would have to do to provide the necessary backing and support for that corporate vision.

As an example, suppose there was a hypothetical company that had a mission to create the most advanced autonomous driving vehicles in the world. The first question organizational leaders might ask is: how, precisely, can the organization's workforce help the company to achieve its goal of creating the most advanced autonomous driving vehicles in the world? Now, suppose the answer to this question lies in providing the company with the most talented engineers in the world with the most specialized skills required to develop the most advanced autonomous driving vehicles in the world. Armed with the knowledge that the organization will need elite skill sets to execute on its corporate mission, organizational leaders now can start to ask questions regarding how the proposed SWP function can help the organization to build and grow a workforce with these required skills. To help guide this discussion, organizational leaders potentially could ask the following questions:

- Can the SWP function provide insight into specifically how many of these elite employees will be required today and in the future?

- Can the SWP function provide insight into the talent supply of these skills in the external talent market?

- Can the SWP function provide tracking and metrics regarding the degree of impact the workforce is having on helping the organization to achieve its mission?

The answers to these questions should provide the organization's leaders with enough information to craft a basic vision, and help them to start thinking through the specific requirements regarding the skills, processes and technology that should be in place to achieve the vision's objectives.

Narrowing the focus of the vision

Once the primary vision is in place, organizational leaders can start to refine the vision and make it more focused. This stage of creating the vision involves asking more clarifying questions on its specifics. These questions will provide more details regarding the tactical components of how the SWP function will help to support the broader corporate vision. What this entails is taking the questions from the previous section and adding follow-up questions that seek answers on specifically how the SWP function will support the organization in the areas outlined below:

- Can the SWP function provide specific insights into how many of these elite employees will be required today and in the future? If yes, how will the function do this?
- Can the SWP function provide insights into talent supply in the external talent market? If yes, how will the function provide these insights?
- Can the SWP function provide tracking and metrics regarding the degree of impact the workforce is having on helping the organization to achieve its mission? If so, how will the SWP function help the organization to establish and track these metrics?

From the questions answered in the broad vision creation and the follow-up clarification questions answered in this section, organizational leaders should have enough information to develop an initial draft of the development of the vision.

Mission validation and socialization

This step of creating the vision involves engaging additional stakeholders and organizational leaders to validate and gather feedback on the initial draft of the vision. This activity will serve two purposes: first, it will begin to build awareness across the organization concerning the SWP function's role as a support mechanism to help the workforce support the broader corporate mission. Second, it will be the initial introduction to the change management component of building an SWP function. There will be a more detailed discussion on this later in the book, but the objective with this is to involve key stakeholders and cross-functional partners in the earlier stages of the upfront development of the mission and foundational aspects of building an SWP function. Engaging with these stakeholders in the earlier stages of the process will provide them with agency in the process and make them feel more involved in the whole design, implementation and execution of the SWP functional roll-out. Gaining this early support is important because it can significantly reduce future resistance to the change that creating a new function like this can sometimes present to the organization and its cross-functional partners.

Building the SWP team

Perhaps the most critical success factor in building a high-powered SWP function is creating a team with the right mix of skills, competencies and experience required to support that function's vision (see Figure 11.3). This is crucial because ultimately it will be the individual members of this team who will be performing the necessary actions required to execute on and deliver the SWP vision. For example, if

Figure 11.3   Building an SWP team requires the right mix of skills, competencies and knowledge

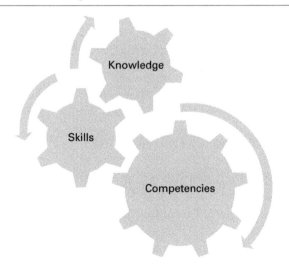

the vision for the SWP function is to 'provide guidance on optimizing the future structure of the workforce' and to do so requires creating sophisticated optimization models, the team will need practitioners who have the skills to build optimization models. If the team does not have this skill set available, however, it will be impossible for it to execute on and achieve its vision. It is for this reason that it is so crucial for organizational leaders to consider the composition of the SWP team in the context of what that team will be expected to achieve.

A useful framework to leverage when creating the talent profiles of the SWP team is to use the analytics maturity curve discussed earlier in this book (see Chapter 10). The workforce analytics maturity curve (see Figure 11.4) is useful in this context because the specific skills that leaders should be thinking about regarding vision alignment and level of impact are typically analytical. The earlier example of needing employees with the ability to create optimization models is a good illustration of this. The following section will provide an overview of how the different stages of the workforce analytics maturity curve relate to and are also applicable to the maturation level of the SWP function. This section will also highlight some of the key skills that are typically required at each stage of the maturity curve.

Basic reporting

Basic reporting is the foundational phase of the workforce analytics maturity curve. In this phase, organizations typically are compiling basic reports from an HRIS data warehouse. The structure of these reports is generally raw data in the form of an Excel spreadsheet. Basic reporting is also an essential aspect of SWP because the SWP function will rely heavily on raw data and reports as a starting point for many of the workforce-related analyses that will be conducted. The skills required are:

- SQL;
- Excel;
- database administration.

Figure 11.4 Maturity curve of an SWP function

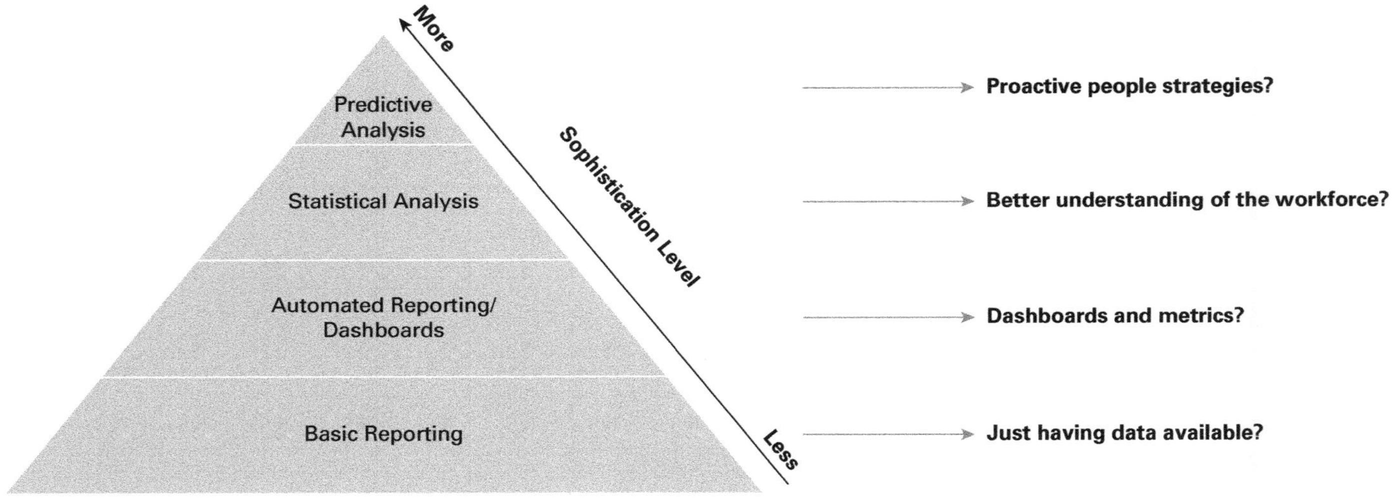

More

Sophistication Level

Less

Predictive Analysis

Statistical Analysis

Automated Reporting/ Dashboards

Basic Reporting

Proactive people strategies?

Better understanding of the workforce?

Dashboards and metrics?

Just having data available?

Dashboarding and metrics reporting

This stage can be characterized by the creation of pivot tables, dashboards and more robust reporting. At this stage of the maturity curve, the objective goes from simply compiling basic reports to transforming and manipulating the data and content of those reports into charts, tables and visualizations that provide more intuitive insight into different dimensions of the workforce. A large component of SWP involves measuring and tracking the health and progress of the organization's workforce against the workforce strategy and Strategic Workforce Plan that the SWP function has created. Measuring and tracking are accomplished through dashboards and metrics reporting. The skills required are:

- SQL;
- Excel;
- database administration;
- data visualization;
- business acumen;
- consulting;
- presentation skills.

Descriptive analytics

As opposed to the first two stages of the maturity curve that dealt with creating basic reports and dashboards from HRIS systems data, the descriptive insights stage is more focused on analysing the underlying data. In this stage, the organization begins to place a greater emphasis on determining and analysing the root cause of and factors that may be contributing to workforce-related events or trends that are impacting on the business. Because SWP involves assessing the current state of the workforce against a desired future state, it is important for the SWP function to be able to understand events that are happening in the current workforce that could impact on the success of the future workforce. The skills required are:

- SQL;
- Excel;

- database administration;
- data visualization;
- business acumen;
- consulting;
- presentation skills;
- statistical analysis;
- data curiosity.

Predictive insights

The final stage of the workforce analytics maturity curve jumps from descriptive analytics, where the analyst is using statistical techniques to try and understand why a workforce-related event happened, to prescriptive analytics where the analyst is now attempting to predict what will occur in the future. For the SWP function, this is the stage of the workforce analytics maturity curve that might be the most important. The reason for this is because, at the most fundamental level, SWP seeks to understand what, if any, gaps exist between the current state of an organization's workforce and some desired future state. For the SWP function to be able to assess this gap requires predicting potential future scenarios. For the SWP function to be able to predict these scenarios requires the function to have an aptitude towards predictive analytics. The skills required are:

- SQL;
- Excel;
- database administration;
- data visualization;
- business acumen;
- consulting;
- presentation skills;
- statistical analysis;
- data curiosity;
- machine learning;
- forecasting.

Understanding the different stages of the workforce analytics maturity curve, the skills required at each stage of the maturity curve and how the stages relate to the maturation and sophistication level of the SWP function is useful for thinking through the skills requirements and composition of the SWP function. That said, this framework tends to become more useful when the organization has already gone through the activity of defining the vision. The reason for this is because, once the vision has been defined, the organization's leaders can quickly refer to the maturity curve to gain insight into what the team members' talent profiles should look like to execute on the vision. As an example, if an organization's SWP vision is to 'provide guidance to organizational leaders on the future hiring requirements at the site, region and global level', it should know there will be a level of predictive analytics that will be required to do this. Armed with this knowledge, the organization can then refer to the maturity curve to gain insight into the fact that the SWP team will be likely to require many of the skill sets associated with the predictive insights stage of the maturity curve.

Size of the function

Once organizational leaders have agreed on the particular talent profile and skills that will be required to achieve the SWP vision, some thought should go into what the optimal size for that team should be. Making this decision can be challenging because, usually, the more advanced and impactful the vision for the SWP function the more important the requirement for a larger team with more diverse skill sets. This requirement can be even greater if the organization is attempting to scale and grow the SWP function across multiple sites and business units throughout the organization. Where things start to get challenging for many organizations trying to build up their SWP functions is when they do not have the budget required to create a large enough team to meet the objectives of the earlier defined vision – at least not in the early stages of building the team. If this ends up becoming a reality, the organization may have to refine the vision or extend the timeline on which achievement of that vision realistically can be expected. There will also need to be some thought put into what skills should initially be hired for the team to drive maximum impact. From a prioritization standpoint, organizational leaders may find it helpful to answer some of the following questions:

- What is the biggest immediate workforce-related challenge that an SWP function could help the organization to solve? If the organization could only hire one employee to help solve this challenge, what skills would they need?

- If the organization only had enough budget to hire one person for the SWP team, are there any current roles in the organization that could support that one employee?

- If the organization only has the budget to hire one new SWP team member a year, what skills should that new hire possess given the priority level for the projects and problems that the SWP function could help to solve?

- For organizations that have dispersion across multiple regional or global sites, where should a small or individual SWP team be located? Will that team or individual only focus on the specific site or will they support more than one site? If they are to support more than one site, what is a reasonable amount of impact that the team or individual could expect to achieve?

After organizational leaders have decided upon the initial size and talent profile of the SWP team, the conversation should shift focus to thinking about how the function will operate and scale from a process and systems standpoint.

Establishing processes and systems for an SWP team

Having a plan in place for how the company will organize and operationalize the day-to-day activities that the SWP team works on is another foundational aspect of building an effective and efficient SWP function. Like the other foundational components, developing a systems, process and scalability plan involves some detailed upfront thought and collaboration from the organization's leaders.

The primary questions these leaders should be answering regarding the processes and systems outlined in Figure 11.5 are:

- *Intake and outtake process:* How can the function guarantee that the stakeholders requiring information have a platform and system in place to ask for that information or data? Also, how can the function ensure that the stakeholders requesting information get the information they are looking for in a timely manner, in the format they want, and with enough context to feel comfortable sharing that information with other leaders and cross-functional partners in the organization?

- *Scaling and growth:* How does the organization scale and grow the above intake and outtake process?

- *Prioritization:* How does the SWP team prioritize the projects and analyses on which they work?

- *Corporate strategy planning:* How does the organization incorporate SWP into the ongoing corporate planning process?

The following sections will provide more context concerning how the organization can approach the challenges outlined above. Before exploring this in more detail, however, it is important to note that

Figure 11.5 Factors to consider when establishing processes and systems for an SWP team

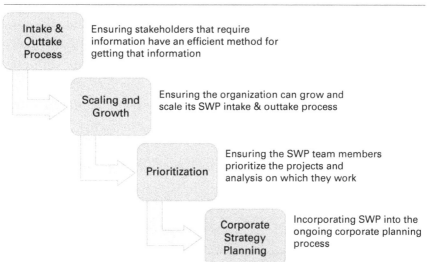

there are micro and macro components to each of these sections. The micro component deals with the team-level output of information, data and insights that the SWP team provides to team leaders. For example, if the SWP team were to conduct a gap analysis on the future impact that attrition might have on the entire organization, the manager of a smaller team would be likely to be only concerned with how that attrition might affect their team. Therefore, rather than asking for the results of the analysis for the entire company, that manager probably would only want to see the data for their team – this is the micro component of the equation. The macro element of that equation, which would be on the opposite side of the spectrum to the micro component, would be more focused on understanding how that attrition might impact on the whole organization and how it might affect the broader corporate strategy. Framing the concept of delivering useful insights, information and data at the micro and macro levels ensures the organization is providing support at both the enterprise and team levels for maximum impact.

Scaling and growth

Scaling and growing the processes and systems that dictate how the SWP function will operate across the business is an important consideration in the upfront design of the function. Once again, the vision of what the SWP function will deliver to the organization will be the guiding principle that drives the degree to which the function will need to scale and grow. If the vision is something as broad as 'providing workforce optimization to drive productivity and efficiency across the enterprise', the function will need to scale and grow significantly. On the other hand, if the vision is less ambitious or more focused on a particular business issue, the need might not be as urgent from a growing and scaling perspective. The most important questions to consider in scaling and growing the SWP function are:

- Which individuals and teams across the organization will require the insights and services the SWP function will provide?
- How often will those individuals and teams require those insights and services?

- How complex are the insights and services that those individuals and teams require?

- Can any of those insights and services be provided to those individuals and teams through some form of self-service technology?

Answering these questions will be the initial step in designing the technology and service delivery model that will help to facilitate the necessary scaling and growth for the SWP vision. The following sections will discuss potential options for this service delivery model.

Intake and outtake process

The first big challenge organizational leaders need to solve regarding the systems and processes that need to be in place for a scalable and efficient SWP function is to think through how the stakeholders can efficiently ask for strategic workforce insights and, furthermore, how the function receives and delivers on these requests. Put another way: how does the SWP function ensure a process is in place to capture and deliver on all the requests that stakeholders are asking for and how does the function establish a process to ensure it is easy for those stakeholders to make and receive those requests? The following questions can help leaders to gain a better understanding of how the SWP function should be structured to meet the intake and outtake process requirements:

- Who are the stakeholders who will be asking for strategic workforce insights?

- Are there primary, secondary and ad hoc stakeholders? What are the criteria that differentiate the different types of stakeholders?

- What is the frequency with which the primary and secondary stakeholders are likely to ask for strategic workforce insights?

- Are there common themes in the types of data and insights that interested parties are likely to request?

- How do the types of requests vary by site, region and country?

- Is there a definitive prioritization matrix in place for which stakeholders and projects receive deliverables first?

- How comfortable are managers and leaders with data and the concepts behind SWP insights? Will these managers and leaders require high levels of support to interpret results and make action-able decisions?

- How does the organization conduct ongoing SWP? For exam-ple, are there weekly, monthly or quarterly meetings that should include an SWP representative?

- How do senior leaders like to receive enterprise-level workforce insights? Do these leaders like to gain insights through a 'push' struc-ture where they might get a summarized report at some ongoing interval or do they like more of a 'pull' structure where they reach out directly to the SWP function when they need specific insights?

Going through the activity of answering these questions will provide valuable information regarding the most optimal approach to take for structuring the SWP intake and outtake processes. When the actual time comes to make a final decision on the intake and outtake process structures, there are a few designs that can be useful to consider.

Ticket tracking request model

In a ticket request system, the stakeholder requesting information sends an e-mail to the SWP team. In this e-mail, they outline the specifics of what they would like to receive and when they would like to receive it. It is important to note that the request they are sending is not to a particular individual but rather the team as a whole. Once received, these requests are then triaged by the SWP team based on the type of request, the level of complexity, the stakeholder initiating the request and the priority of the request. After the team has triaged the request, they should provide a response to the stakeholder who initiated the request that outlines a timeframe for when they will receive the required information along with a summary of exactly what the SWP team will provide to that stakeholder in the final deliverable. The organization should address several other clarifying details before implementing a ticket tracking request system:

- What criteria should be used to prioritize and triage the requests? Who are the stakeholders that should be involved in developing these criteria?

- Who will handle the triaging of ticketed requests? Will this be handled by one individual on the team or multiple team members?

- What degree of familiarity should the individual handling the requests have regarding the requestor and the specific request (in reality, the individual handling the request should have a solid understanding of the business, stakeholders and underlying criteria used to triage the requests)?

- Will there be follow-up support provided in addition to the original deliverable? If so, who will be providing the follow-up support?

- How will the effectiveness and service level support of the ticket tracking request system be measured? For example, will there be follow-up e-mails or surveys soliciting feedback on how well the ticketed request process worked?

Embedded support model

The ticket tracking request system provides the organization with SWP intake and outtake processes that form more of a centralized centre of excellence (COE) approach in the delivery of insights. An approach of this nature works best when the types of requests are more simplistic and routine. This method does not work as smoothly, however, when the request for support is for more sophisticated and complex projects and analysis. When the requests take on this form, a closer partnership and consultative approach can be more effective. In an embedded support model, there is usually one member of the SWP team who works directly with a particular stakeholder group to partner with for ongoing support. Because there is one dedicated resource from the SWP team who works directly with the stakeholder group on a day-to-day basis, there will be a more intimate understanding gained by that dedicated resource to address that group's particular workforce-related business challenges. This enhanced understanding of the nuances that make up the stakeholder group's workforce challenges will provide that dedicated resource with better context for providing more customized and detailed solutions to that stakeholder regarding those challenges.

The biggest and most obvious problem with an embedded support model is the difficulty that comes with trying to scale and grow the model. The fundamental idea behind this model is that there should be one dedicated resource for each of the client or stakeholder groups that require support. If there are more than three or four teams that need support (which is probably on the lower end of the support that will be necessary), it is easy to see how the number of resources that would be needed to support a model of this nature could quickly grow into a relatively large team. Most organizations do not have the headcount budget to support an SWP function of this size – especially in the early stages of the function's life cycle.

Mixed ticketed and embedded support model

There are opportunities and challenges for both the ticket tracking and embedded support models. Because of these opportunities and challenges, another possible approach is a mixed model. A mixed model includes elements from both the ticket tracking and embedded support models combined into one. The idea behind a mixed ticket and support model is to provide an option for stakeholders and client groups to have some form of either of these models to choose from depending on the unique situation and operating environment in which the different teams operate. Teams that do not require as much sophistication regarding the insights they are seeking can leverage the ticketed support component of this model, while a few other stakeholder groups that might need more hands-on support can take advantage of the embedded support component of the model. The key to making a mixed ticketed and embedded support model work is going through the upfront exercise first of identifying the stakeholder and client groups that will be leveraging SWP insights and, second, defining the level of support and insights those groups would like to gain from the SWP team.

Once the identification of the stakeholder and client groups is complete, and there is some basic understanding concerning the level of support and insights these groups will require, organizational leaders can create a mixed model structure that prioritizes which teams and groups will get what level of support. Once again, it is important to note that the degree of support and ability to scale intake and outtake processes and systems of this nature will largely be dependent on the amount of resources the SWP function has at its disposal. In other words, it will be challenging for an organization to scale and grow a mixed ticket and embedded support model if the SWP function is made up of one solo practitioner.

Service prioritization

When optimizing the systems and processes that need to be in place for the SWP function to have maximum impact, there should be some thought put into the prioritization of service delivery. Prioritization of this delivery is an important consideration because, as the SWP function begins to grow and have more impact, there is a good chance the demand for the services the function is providing will start to rise exponentially. This growth in demand can lead to challenges with competing priorities. If leaders can agree on a logical system for prioritizing requests and then articulate to the function's stakeholders and partners how requests for analysis, data and support are prioritized, there is likely to be much less disappointment from those stakeholders regarding unmet expectations. A good approach to this prioritization is to develop a prioritization matrix based on some agreed upon principles and criteria. Typically, the criteria that a good priority matrix would include are:

- Who is the client who is requesting support?
- Is the request for support an urgent business need?
- What are the sophistication level and time required for the request?
- Is the request routine or recurring and simpler in nature?

Once the criteria are in place for how to prioritize different requests, there should be an assignment of weights for each of those criteria. The more important criteria should be weighted higher and the less important ones should be rated lower. After the allocation of these weights, the remaining exercise becomes a simple maths activity based on the type of request. For example, a request from a C-suite executive that is in support of an urgent business need would score higher on the priority matrix than a request from a C-suite executive that is not in direct support of an urgent business need.

Corporate strategy planning

An effective SWP team should not only be a team that supports HR and business leaders with answers to questions on optimizing the workforce, but also partner with the business to provide workforce-related inputs to corporate strategic planning. Incorporating SWP into the organization's corporate strategy process involves understanding and outlining how precisely the corporate strategic planning sessions will utilize the workforce strategy and SWP. As a starting point, it is important to agree what part or parts of the workforce strategy and SWP should be included in the corporate strategy. Doing so will guide the SWP team to the areas to focus on for the strategic planning sessions. As an example, if the corporate strategy has a focus on an aggressive expansion plan across multiple sites and regions, the workforce strategy component of that plan might focus primarily on location-based SWP.

After defining how corporate strategy planning will utilize the workforce strategy and Strategic Workforce Plan, it is important to outline when the organization's corporate planning sessions will require SWP inputs. Questions that should be answered regarding the timing of the SWP function's inputs include:

- How often will corporate strategy planning happen?
- Will SWP be included in every strategy planning session?
- For the sessions that involve the SWP function, will there be any pre-work or deliverables that should be completed prior to the sessions?
- If there are deliverables that the SWP function will be required to provide, how much lead time is needed to prepare those deliverables?

Incorporating data and technology into the SWP process

The final foundational component that should be considered in the design of an SWP function is the role that data and technology will play in providing workforce insights to the organization. Not thinking through the data and technology component of the SWP process is another trap that many organizations fall into in the early stages of the SWP journey. The danger of not thinking through this in the initial stages of building out an SWP function risks running into data quality issues with no technology in place to scale the insights the function hopes to provide to the organization.

Data

There should be little debate that, without data, SWP would be little more than an exercise in guesswork, but the SWP function just having data is not enough to be able to provide meaningful insights to the organization. Rather, the data have to be high quality and reliable in nature or risk leading to analyses with conclusions that are erroneous and inaccurate. For this reason, it is imperative that the organization goes through two key data-related activities before formally implementing an SWP function across the organization. These two activities are, first, data quality assessment and, second, inventory analysis on what data the organization currently possesses and what data the organization needs to deliver for robust SWP.

Data quality assessment

The first data-related activity the organization should undertake before moving forward with the implementation of the SWP function involves assessing the quality of the data. Evaluating the quality of the organization's 'people data' is necessary because it is not uncommon for the data housed in the organization's HRIS to be full of mistakes with inaccurate or outdated information. These errors typically stem from two causes. First, because many organizations in the past may not have placed a priority on analysing the workforce, the systems in place that are required to analyse workforce-related data might have been lacking in proper upkeep. Second, because much of the data in HRIS warehouses are derived from manual entries, these manual entries can lead to inconsistencies and errors when it comes to retrieving the data from the organization's HRIS. For obvious reasons, this can be troublesome when attempting to perform a thorough analysis. These two confounding factors are why it becomes essential for the organization to conduct a data quality assessment.

When going through this evaluation, the organization should be paying particular attention to the following areas:

- What are the fields in the HRIS data warehouse that require manual entries? How much variance is possible for those inputted entries? For example, if there is a requirement for the recruiters to input where a candidate attended university, is it possible for one recruiter to input 'U of Michigan' and another to input 'University of Michigan'?

- Mergers, acquisitions and changes in the organizational structure (reorganization): Have there been any reorganizations that might have impacted on hierarchies in the data?

- Are there data fields and tables in the HRIS warehouse that have been deprecated? Are these deprecated fields and tables leading to confusion?

- Regulations and compliance: Are there different data regulations and compliance factors at the country or region level that can impact on the data's consistency?

- Are definitions in place that define what the data are and from where they have come? If not, it is important for this information to become available. Anytime an analysis is conducted, the analyst performing it should be able to answer any questions that might arise regarding the data's origin.

The data assessment should be comprehensive enough so there is accountability for each column and row of data in the data warehouse. Going through this activity can be a daunting task, which is why it is important to have an analyst in place who can use programming languages like SQL and Python to quickly summarize and review the tables, columns and rows for the mistakes and errors discussed thus far.

Once the data assessment is complete, a list should be compiled of all the tables and fields in the data warehouse that possess inconsistencies and errors. From there, an action plan should be developed to reconcile these issues. In addition to this reconciliation, a plan should be put in place that outlines how the data will be audited and maintained in the future and by whom.

Data inventory assessment

In addition to assessing the quality of data, it is also important to understand the variety of data that the organization possesses. Understanding the range of data is important because it will provide the organization with insights into the different types of analysis that the SWP function potentially can perform. It will also shed light on where the SWP analyst might face limitations due to a lack of data. Finally, it can help the organization to understand the types of data that it will need to acquire in the future to provide more comprehensive insights to organizational leaders.

Fortunately, performing the data inventory assessment can be done in tandem with the data quality assessment. Accomplishing this can be achieved by creating a list of all the data fields that were assessed during the data quality assessment. Once the creation of this list is complete, organizational leaders can then evaluate the data fields contained in the list against the relevance of them to the SWP function. Going through this part of the data inventory assessment is especially useful because it can also shed light on missing HRIS data fields that might be helpful for certain analysis that the SWP function might perform. Once these missing data fields have been identified, organizational leaders can then shift their focus to begin thinking through if and how the organization might collect the data for those missing data fields. It can also lead to discussions about the limitations that the SWP function could potentially face – from an analytics standpoint – if it is not possible to collect those missing data.

Technology

Technology is the final factor that should be considered when putting the foundational building blocks in place to create an effective SWP function. Technology in the context of scaling and growing an SWP function refers to the tools that will be used to analyse and visualize data, creating self-service capabilities for key stakeholders and the platform from which the insights will be delivered to the organization. As illustrated in Figure 11.6, the key factors that should be assessed for each of the possible technology solutions are:

- cost of the technology;
- scalability of the technology;
- usability of the technology;
- sophistication level of the technology;
- skills required to use the technology.

Figure 11.6 Factors to consider when deciding on a technology solution for an SWP function

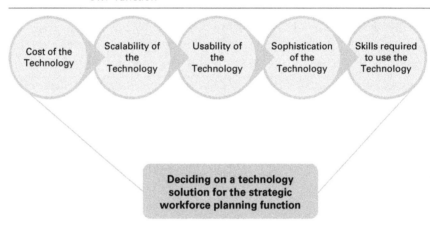

Technology to analyse and visualize data

There are various tools on the market that the SWP function can leverage to analyse and visualize data. These tools vary in their cost, ease of use and sophistication levels. As outlined below, there are essentially three different categories that technological solutions fall into.

Basic technology solutions

Spreadsheets are the most basic and flexible tool that the SWP function can utilize to analyse and visualize data. Spreadsheets are relatively cheap and, in some cases, free (Google Sheets is a free cloud-based spreadsheet service offered by Google). Microsoft Excel is a very popular spreadsheet for which many organizations already have licences, which can make it an attractive option. It is also so widely used in the business world that it is not uncommon for company employees to have at least a basic knowledge of how to use an Excel spreadsheet. Spreadsheets provide the SWP practitioner with a platform to create tables and charts, organize and summarize data, perform statistical analysis, visualize data and finally share the results of the data and analysis with stakeholders and clients. Because spreadsheets are so commonly used and easy to share for most organizations, this is a simple but effective option not only as a primary starting point, but also as a scalability solution. The downside of spreadsheets is that there is still a significant amount of manual work required. Performing more sophisticated analysis also can be challenging, and will be likely to need more advanced skills to utilize the spreadsheet's more advanced functions, which is something that also should be a consideration.

Intermediate technology solutions

The next category of technology tools that can potentially be an option for the SWP function to use for analytics and visualization comprise cloud-based business intelligence solutions such as Tableau, IBM Watson Analytics, Visier and Microsoft Power BI. The attractiveness of these technology solutions is the ease of use, visualization capabilities, automated dashboard creation and ability to synthesize and summarize disparate data sources with the touch of a button. In recent years, some of these technologies have transformed from being tools used primarily for data visualization and dashboard creation to platforms that provide more statistical and prescriptive insights.

The downside of these technologies typically relates to their cost compared to the other options. The cost challenges of these options are exacerbated for larger organizations, which is to say, as the size of the organization grows, the cost of obtaining licences from one of these vendors can grow substantially. The other challenge with these tools deals with the transparency of the back-end calculations and dashboard creations. The issue here is that, because the development of some of the calculations and dashboards happens on the back end of the platform, there can be a perception that they are created in a black box, which can make explaining and defending them to clients and stakeholders more difficult.

Because choosing one of these vendors can be a substantial investment for an organization and the solution that they provide can make or break the organization's ability to scale and grow the SWP function, it is worth reviewing the vendor selection framework discussed earlier in this book. Criteria to include in the external workforce insights vendor assessment process are listed below.

Customer service   When it comes to the relationship between the vendor and the organization using the vendor's services a true partnership should exist. What that means is a vendor should be in place that is responsive and provides excellent customer service. If the organization is going to invest a significant amount of money on a workforce insights solution, that organization should expect the provider to understand the company, listen to the company's concerns and be willing to be flexible to meet the dynamic nature in which most organizations operate.

Systems integration   The ability for the chosen software to seamlessly integrate with the organization's current systems and data warehouses should be one of the first questions asked of the vendor. They should be able to accurately identify which systems can be integrated, how that integration will take place, how long the integration will take and any risks associated with the systems integration.

Data privacy   Data privacy is probably the biggest risk factor an organization can face when partnering with an external vendor for workforce insights. Because this is such a huge area of concern for most organizations, it is important to ensure that vendors are assessed on their ability to make sure that all confidential employee data will be highly secured in the software offering. There should be significant detail provided on how the vendor will make sure that there will be no data privacy risk with their software.

Analytics   The big question that leaders should seek answers to here relates to the level of sophistication that the software can provide from an analytics standpoint. To that end, is the software only providing data summarization and visualization or are there more prescriptive and predictive components to the solution? If the vendor claims to offer predictive and prescriptive components in their offering, can they describe the maths behind their claims?

Technology usability Another consideration is the usability of the technology. If the software is such that it is too complicated for the end user to figure out, much of the value that is supposed to be derived from it will be lost. Because of this, it is important to assess the software's user interface for usability. Ultimately, the vendor should provide a technology that drives adoption across the organization. A clunky or awkward-to-use tool can be intimidating for end users and ultimately end up being more of a hindrance than a valuable option for the organization.

References The final aspect to include as assessment criteria are references or customer reviews. Having the vendor provide the organization with references is a crucial element to understanding the strengths and weaknesses of the product or service. Customer references are so important that it makes sense to try and get them from both the vendor and independent third-party sources. Taking a two-pronged approach will ensure the reviews received are not biased from a vendor-centric standpoint.

Advanced technology solutions

Finally, there is the more advanced category of technology solutions to create and deliver workforce insights. The advanced category includes statistical tools like R, Python, SAS and STATA that provide a platform for the SWP practitioner to conduct more advanced statistical analysis. The first thing to consider with these tools is whether or not the vision for the SWP function will require the level of statistical sophistication that these tools can provide. This is an important consideration because there is a certain degree of skill that is required to be able to use these tools. If the organization is not planning on providing more sophisticated predictive modelling as part of the end vision for the SWP function, there is probably no reason to include them in the context of the technology strategy.

If the organization's vision does include more sophisticated predictive analysis in its end vision, then statistical tools and software of this nature will be imperative. The most significant trade-off to think about regarding these tools is the cost versus usability factor.

Considering this is important because some of the software in this category is open source while others are subscription based. The big trade-off is that the open-source solutions are free, but require the analyst to have significant skills and experience with programming languages to be able to use them. The subscription-based tools tend to be much easier to use with far fewer programming requirements.

There are many details to think about regarding the data and technology strategy the SWP function will use. The decisions the company makes regarding these details are very important and can have a significant impact on the organization's ability to scale and provide consistent, accurate and actionable workforce insights through its SWP function. For this reason, it is important to go through the above activities with much care, focus and thought before making any finalized decisions regarding the function's data and technology strategy.

Summary of chapter objectives

The importance of building a foundation for an SWP function

Before going through the process of implementing an SWP function, it is critical that the organization creates a foundation on which the function can stand. Without this foundation in place, the function risks not having the structure, processes and mission necessary to scale, grow and drive the value that the SWP process has the potential to create. There are essentially four key foundational pillars the organization should consider in the design phase of an SWP team:

1 What is the vision for the SWP team?

2 Who needs to be on the SWP team and what skills do they require?

3 What are the systems and processes that need to be in place to scale the SWP team?

4 What are the technology and data requirements that need to be in place for the SWP team to deliver actionable insights?

Crafting a vision for the SWP function

The first consideration in building a high-powered SWP function is the vision for the function. It is very important to go through the process of developing a vision for the SWP function because this essentially is the starting point to build the function's other foundational pillars. Creating a vision for the SWP function also provides leaders with an end point to the journey on which the organization is about to embark. That is to say, the vision is essentially the end goal for what the SWP function hopes to achieve. If everything goes smoothly, the vision represents a successful SWP implementation. That said, developing a vision for the SWP function involves three key areas:

1 thinking through how the SWP function will contribute to the success of the company's broader mission;

2 narrowing in on the focus of the vision;

3 socialization and validation of the vision.

Building the SWP team

Once the vision is in place, it is important to start thinking about how the team will be structured to efficiently execute on that vision. This essentially involves thinking through the skills, experience, education and leadership that will be required of that team to realize the vision that has been set forth by the organization for the SWP function. A useful framework to leverage when creating the talent profiles for the SWP team is to use the workforce analytics maturity curve that was discussed in Chapter 10. This framework is particularly useful because maturation of the workforce analytics maturity curve, from a skills standpoint, tends to mirror the primary skills that will be required for organizations that are more aspirational in their vision for their SWP functions. That is to say, if organizations want to get to a point where their SWP process is helping to deliver optimized future states for their workforces, they will be likely to require a fairly sophisticated mix of skills ranging from consulting to statistics to change management and leadership. As a reminder, the primary skills required at the most mature phase of the workforce analytics maturity curve include:

- SQL;
- Excel;
- database administration;
- data visualization;
- business acumen;
- consulting;
- presentation skills;
- statistics;
- data curiosity;
- machine learning;
- forecasting.

Establishing processes and systems for an SWP team

Another key component for the organization to think about regarding the creation of an SWP function is how this new function will interact with the rest of the organization to deliver actionable, scalable and timely insights. To have an SWP function that is able to deliver on this objective requires thinking about the processes and systems that will need to be agreed on and in place as the Strategic Workforce Plan is launched and integrated with the rest of the business. There are certain questions that leaders should be discussing and deciding upon that will help to surface some of the key considerations regarding these systems and processes. Some of these questions include:

- *Intake and outtake process:* How can the function guarantee that the stakeholders requiring information have a platform and system in place to ask for that information or data? Also, how can the function ensure that the stakeholders requesting information get the information they are looking for in a timely manner, in the format they want, and with enough context to feel comfortable sharing the information with other leaders and cross-functional partners in the organization?

- *Scaling and growth:* How does the organization scale and grow the above intake and outtake process?

- *Prioritization:* How does the SWP team prioritize the projects and analyses on which they work?
- *Corporate strategy planning:* How does the organization incorporate SWP into the ongoing corporate planning process?

Incorporating data and technology into the SWP process

The final foundational component that should be considered in the design of an SWP function is the role that data and technology will play in providing workforce insights to the organization. Not thinking through the data and technology component of the SWP process is another trap that many organizations fall into in the early stages of the SWP journey. The danger of not thinking through this in the initial stages of building out an SWP function risks running into data quality issues with no technology in place to scale the insights the function hopes to provide to the organization.

Conclusion

This chapter has provided an overview of the key foundational components that should be planned out before launching and implementing an SWP function. It cannot be stressed enough how important it is for business and HR leaders to spend a significant amount of upfront time deliberating on the details of these foundational components. If done correctly with enough thought and planning, the organization will have the necessary pillars forged to build a high-powered, sustainable and scalable SWP function that will be a partner with the business in creating value and improving company performance.

The role of change management in strategic workforce planning

12

CHAPTER OBJECTIVES

1 Define change management.
2 Outline the importance of change management in SWP.
3 Outline key steps in creating a change-management plan for the SWP function.

Change management

Heraclitus, the pre-Socratic Greek philosopher, is famous for coining the phrase: 'change is the only constant in life'. Heraclitus's statement is broadly applicable not only regarding human life but also across other relevant topics such as the evolution of business and technology. Change is so important in business that, when organizations do not embrace it, they risk being rendered obsolete by competitors who may be using it as a tool to adapt and innovate their business models. Furthermore, with the advancement of technology increasing at exponential rates, the importance of change, or rather adapting to change, has become so critical for many organizations that it is often factored into their long-term corporate strategies.

If change is so prevalent and common in both life and business, why do certain people and organizations have such a difficult time embracing it? The answer is that there is no one particular factor that makes adapting to change more challenging for some than others. Rather, there is a combination of factors that lead to our resistance to change. Steve McKee's 2009 publication, entitled *When Growth Stalls*, outlines some of these factors. For starters, once we forge habits and norms into our brains, it can become difficult to 'change' or overcome these habits. Our brains also tend to be hardwired to resist change because change involves learning new things. Learning new things requires our brains (the pre-frontal cortex to be exact) to use more energy, which means more effort or difficulty that ultimately leads to more resistance. There is also a natural desire for us to learn experientially. Doing or experiencing something new makes our brains much more open to learning. Typically, when we resist change, we have not yet gone through the process of experiencing and doing, which is so crucial in adapting to change.

Kurt Lewin is famous for writing on the topic of resistance to change being an almost inevitable social construct in the organizational environment for most companies (Lewin, 2008). If this is true, what can organizations do to mitigate against the risk that comes with the disruption associated with this resistance to change? Before this question can be answered, it is important to understand what change means in the context of business. From a strictly business standpoint, change can refer to the introduction of a new process, system, project, technology or operating procedure. At some point, most organizations' employees will be involved or interact with these, and they all require some degree of change or adoption. It is natural that there will be some level of resistance to change as these employees attempt to learn and process what these changes will mean to them and the way they conduct their work. An organization can mitigate against the risk associated with this change by developing a change-management strategy and plan. At its most simple level, change management refers to the systems, tools and frameworks used by organizations to help employees and teams more easily adapt to change.

In the last 30 years, there has been considerable research in the field of change management. Academics and practitioners have studied change, and the impact and disruption it can have on organizations and their business operations, with the hope of developing some frameworks and models that these organizations can use to reduce the resistance to change. From this research, some notable models have been developed that have proven useful in helping organizations to structure and operationalize their approach to managing the resistance to change. Some of these more popular models include the following.

Kurt Lewin's unfreeze-change-refreeze model

Kurt Lewin is best known for being one of the early pioneers of modern industrial psychology. He is also famous for producing one of the first and most popular frameworks for dealing with change called the unfreeze-change-refreeze model. This is a three-stage model in which the first stage involves preparing for the change. The second stage includes the inter-movement of transition that individuals experience as they go through the change. Finally, the third stage deals with creating a sense of stability once the change has been made and is finalized (Weick and Quinn, 1999).

ADKAR®

The ADKAR® model was developed by Jeff Hiatt during his tenure as the CEO of Prosci®. The model was first introduced in 2003 and follows a sequential framework aimed at facilitating change at the individual level. The steps included in Hiatt's model are:

1 awareness of the need for change;
2 desire to participate in and support the change;
3 knowledge of how to change;
4 ability to implement desired skills and behaviours;
5 reinforcement to sustain the change.

The ADKAR® model is famous for being more practical and simplistic, which makes it a popular choice for organizations looking for a simple change-management framework to support their strategies in the early stages of developing a change-management strategy (Hiatt, 2006).

John Kotter's eight-step process of change

John Kotter introduced the original John Kotter eight-step process of change in 1996 in his book entitled *Leading Change*. He has since expanded on the framework in another book: *Accelerate: Building Strategic Agility for a Faster-Moving World* (Kotter, 2014). Kotter's eight-step process of change model focuses on eight critical phases in the change process that, if not executed properly, can lead to suboptimal outcomes regarding the organization's ability to manage change (Kotter and Cohen, 2002). Those eight key areas are:

1 establishing a sense of urgency;

2 creating the guiding coalition;

3 developing a vision and strategy;

4 communicating the change vision;

5 empowering broad-based action;

6 generating short-term wins;

7 consolidating wins and producing more change;

8 anchoring new approaches in the culture.

The importance of change management in SWP

The preceding section introduced the concept of change management along with a few popular frameworks that some organizations use to help guide their change-management strategies. In this section, the discussion will shift focus to the implications of change management for SWP.

While the basic concept of SWP may seem relatively intuitive in theory, taking this concept and turning it into a formalized principle that is part of how the company operates can be a little more abstract. On the journey that takes the concept of SWP from being theoretical to becoming part of the organization's DNA is where the value of change management becomes crucial to the long-term success of the SWP function. As with the introduction of any other new process, project or method of working, the organization as a whole and, more specifically, the stakeholders that will be impacted by this new approach to conducting business, probably will display some form of resistance in the early stages of the function's implementation. The degree to which this resistance will impact on the ability of the SWP team to gain momentum and deliver positive results will be a function of how well the organization can contain this resistance to change.

There are several key areas in particular where change management can be especially beneficial in the implementation and roll-out of the SWP function. The following sections will discuss in more detail the benefits of a reliable change-management strategy for the three key areas identified in Figure 12.1.

Establishing the roles, responsibilities and interdependencies of the SWP function

As has been discussed throughout this book, a good SWP function does not operate in a silo. What this means is the SWP function should partner with the different teams across the business to provide insights that are tailored to the requirements that make each of these teams unique. Doing so, however, requires the SWP team to understand who the stakeholders are and what their specific level of involvement should be in the SWP process. It is in this part of the

Figure 12.1   There are three key areas that can lead to resistance to change

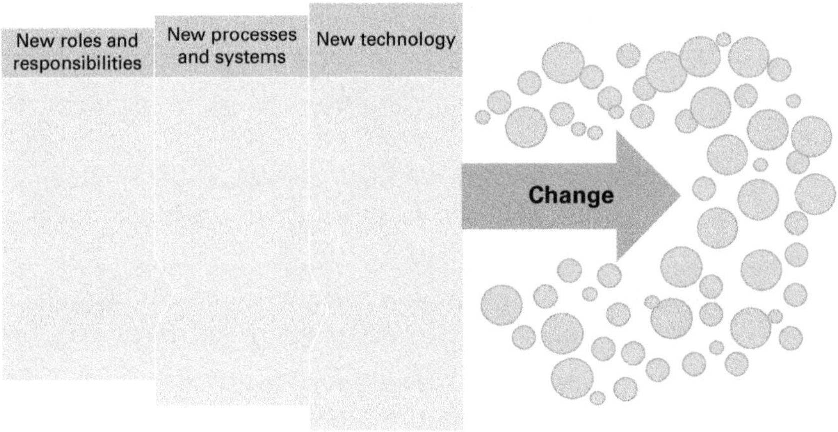

New roles and responsibilities

New processes and systems

New technology

Change

process that change management can be a useful tool for the SWP practitioner. The reason why change management can be beneficial in this scenario is that the individuals and stakeholders that the SWP practitioner will be trying to form partnerships with probably will not understand the intention of the partnership and what value it will offer to them in exchange for their time and resources. Going through the change-management process can help to alleviate some of the potential resistance that these stakeholders and individuals might feel when being introduced to the concept of SWP for the first time.

Introducing new processes and systems to scale and grow the potential impact of the SWP function

Potentially one of the biggest areas where the SWP function might face resistance is in the initial stages of the development and implementation of new processes and systems that will need to be in place for the function to be effective. As outlined earlier in this chapter, there is a natural tendency for people to be resistant to new concepts with which they are not familiar. Understanding these new concepts, including new operating procedures, processes and systems, requires more mental energy, which can lead to a less-comfortable mental state. Not surprisingly, there is a natural tendency to fight or resist this uncomfortable mental state. When an SWP function is being introduced and implemented for the first time, there will be many new processes and systems that certain stakeholders will have to learn and become familiar with. It is no wonder that the introduction of these new SWP processes and systems potentially can lead to resistance across the organization. A good change-management strategy once again can make the transition to these new processes and systems much smoother.

Implementing technology support systems for the SWP function

Another pillar of SWP that has the potential to be disruptive to the organization is the implementation and adoption of the technology involved in scaling and growing the SWP function. When organizations make the decision to adopt a new technology, several change-management factors should be considered regarding the implementation of that technology:

- Who are the stakeholders, teams and individuals that will be using the technology?
- How often will these stakeholders, teams and individuals use the technology?
- How complicated or sophisticated is the new technology?
- Will the new technology require training? If so, how much training will it require?
- Who are the stakeholders that will need to be involved in the implementation and roll-out of the technology? How much of these stakeholders' time will be required for the implementation and roll-out of the new technology?
- How long will the implementation and roll-out of the new technology take?
- How will the organization ensure the technology is adopted? Who will be held accountable for this adoption?

The questions raised above are also directly applicable to the SWP function in the implementation and roll-out of the technology and systems that will be needed to support and scale workforce-related insights. Based on some of the factors that have been discussed in the chapter thus far regarding resistance to change, the questions raised above also have the potential to be disruptive to the organization in that introduction and implementation phase of the technology. It should be no surprise then that change management will be a significant factor in the SWP function's ability to successfully implement and adopt the new technology.

Creating a change-management plan for the SWP function

Designing, implementing, growing and scaling an SWP function will introduce the organization to a substantial number of new concepts, processes, systems and technologies. All these factors have the potential to lead to significant disruption in the organization. If not dealt with appropriately, this disruption can lead to the function not delivering on what it was intended to provide, or worse, result in a failed implementation that costs the organization valuable time and resources. Therefore, it is critical that the organization develops a change-management plan to help facilitate and guide the introduction and implementation of the SWP function. This section will provide SWP practitioners and organizational leaders with some steps that can assist in the development of a practical and useful change-management plan to help reduce some of that disruption (see Figure 12.2).

Purpose

The first critical component of an effective change-management plan is to outline the purpose of the plan. The level of detail that goes into defining the purpose of the plan will be dependent upon the complexity, size and scope of the underlying organizational change the plan is being created to address. With that in mind, the purpose statement can be as simple as one sentence or as long as a full paragraph.

Describe the change

The next step in a robust SWP change-management plan is a section that outlines the specifics of what is happening with the SWP

Figure 12.2 Steps required to develop an SWP change-management plan

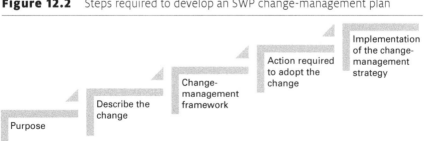

implementation that will change the way in which the organization operates. Considerations that can be highlighted in this section include:

- specifically what the change is;
- the reason for the change; for example, the organization needs to adopt a new analytics technology to provide managers with access to self-service, people-related insights;
- the size and scope of the change;
- a description of the organization's current state and how the change will impact on that current environment;
- what the specific goal or success metric for the change will be;
- a statement regarding how ready the organization is for the change, in other words: what is the anticipated disruption or resistance that the organization could experience due to the change and how prepared is it to deal with that disruption or resistance?

Change-management framework

In this component of the change-management plan, the SWP function provides an overview of the framework that will be used to help facilitate the change. Will the organization use John Kotter's eight-step process of change, Kurt Lewin's unfreeze-change-refreeze model or a hybrid of different models? It will also address who the key stakeholders are along with the roles and responsibilities of the individual or individuals who will be leading the change efforts.

Actions required to adopt the change

This section of the change-management plan outlines more of the specific details that the SWP function will need to consider to deliver on the change-management plan. The level of detail once again will depend on the scale and scope of the change being addressed by the SWP function. Irrespective of the complexity of the change, this section still should be relatively precise on the particular actions that will need to take place to ensure the plan is executed effectively. Some areas that should be outlined in this section include:

- details concerning the steps that the SWP function will need to take to influence the change in the organization; for example, senior-level support and messaging concerning the importance of SWP can be an action step in the change-management plan to help influence the organization;
- details of the specific steps the SWP function will need to take to address and influence process change;
- details of the specific steps the SWP function will take to address and influence people change;
- how the SWP function will share and communicate information regarding the change to teams and stakeholder groups across the organization;
- the potential cost and impact of the change to the organization.

Implementation of the change-management strategy

The final component of a good change-management plan provides guidance on the specific actions the SWP function will have to perform to execute a successful change-management strategy. This portion of the change-management plan will have more content compared to the other sections. Essentially there are four subsections of topics that should be addressed in meticulous detail before the organization formalizes the SWP function's change-management strategy:

- action plan;
- communications plan;
- training plan;
- overcoming resistance plan (ORP).

Action plan

The action plan provides guidance on each of the specific tasks involved in the change-management plan. The action plan should contain clarity on the timeline for completion of each task along with who will be responsible for the task and any dependencies that might be related to it.

Communications plan

One of the biggest factors that can affect the SWP function's ability to build support, gain momentum and overcome resistance is communicating to stakeholders the impact that the SWP function and associated change will have on them. Because communication is so important in the change-management process, it is critical to have a communications plan in place that outlines how the organization will communicate the objectives of the SWP function, when these communications will happen, how the communication will be delivered and specifically to whom the communications will be addressed. A good communications plan will run in tandem with the broader change-management plan.

Training plan

Because the SWP function will introduce the organization to new processes, systems and technologies, there will be a need for the SWP function's stakeholders to learn them. The most effective way to help ensure these stakeholders are adequately trained on these new processes, systems and technologies is to develop a training plan. The change-management training plan should outline the specifics of what is to be learned, who will have to learn it, how it will be taught and how the learning objectives of the training plan will be measured.

Overcoming resistance plan (ORP)

The ORP is a proactive artefact included in the broader change-management plan that will provide the SWP function with guidance on how to address various types of resistance. The ORP should outline different scenarios regarding potential opposition that could be caused by the change associated with the different process, people and technology components that will be introduced through the new SWP function. Through these scenarios, the ORP should provide strategies and concrete steps for how to deal with the resistance that may arise throughout the SWP implementation process.

Summary of chapter objectives

Change management

At its most simple level, change management refers to the systems, tools and frameworks used by organizations to help employees and teams adapt more quickly to change. As competition in the business world has steadily increased over the last several decades, so too has the importance for organizations to recognize the need to have systems and processes in place to manage the change and resistance associated with this hyper-competitive landscape. The resultant acknowledgement by organizations of the need to manage change has led to an increase in academic research on the topic of change management. From this research, some notable models have been developed that have proven useful in helping organizations to structure and operationalize their approach to managing the resistance to change. Some of the more popular models are:

- Kurt Lewin's unfreeze-change-refreeze model;
- ADKAR®;
- John Kotter's eight-step process of change.

The importance of change management in SWP

As has been discussed throughout this book, a good SWP function does not operate in a silo. What this means is the SWP function should partner with the different teams across the business to provide insights that are tailored to the requirements that make each of these teams unique. Doing so, however, requires the SWP team to understand who the stakeholders are and what their specific level of involvement should be in the SWP process. It is in this part of the process that change management can be a useful tool for the SWP practitioner. The reason why change management can be beneficial in this scenario is that the individuals and stakeholders that the SWP practitioner will be reaching out to form partnerships with probably will not understand the intention of the partnership and what value it will offer to them in exchange for their time and resources. Going through the change-management process can help to alleviate some of the potential resistance that these stakeholders and individuals might express when being introduced to the concept of SWP for the first time.

Creating a change-management plan for the SWP function

Implementing and rolling out a new SWP function has the potential to lead to a significant amount of disruption across the organization. This is mainly because designing, implementing, growing and scaling an SWP function will introduce the organization to a substantial number of new concepts, processes, systems and technologies. If not dealt with appropriately, this disruption can lead to the function not delivering on what it was intended to provide, or worse, result in a failed implementation that costs the organization valuable time and resources. Therefore, it is critical that the organization develops a change-management plan to help facilitate and guide the introduction and implementation of the SWP function. There are several critical components relating to change management in an SWP function's roll-out that should include considerable deliberation by organizational leaders as part of the creation of the SWP function's change-management strategy:

- describing the purpose of the change-management plan;
- outlining the change that will need to take place in the organization;
- actions required to adopt the change;
- implementation plan for the change-management strategy.

Resistance to change is often considered to be a natural part of the organizational environment in most organizations. This resistance to change in and of itself probably would not be a big deal if it were to happen only occasionally. The problem is, however, that this change does not just happen occasionally. In fact, this change is practically constant for most organizations. It is this constant state of change and the resistance that comes with that change that makes change management so important for most organizations. This is especially so for the SWP process in most organizations where, for the vast majority of employees and leaders, SWP might be an entirely new concept. This is why the SWP function should have a solid change-management plan in place as the function grows and scales across the business.

Strategic workforce planning for the future of work

CHAPTER OBJECTIVES

1 Describe how the landscape of work is changing.

2 Describe the role of technology in the changing landscape of work.

3 Describe the role of SWP in the future of work.

How the landscape of work is changing

One of the key themes that was discussed in the last chapter dealt with the fact that change is inevitable both in life and in business. The concept of change being constant is particularly true when it comes to thinking about how work has changed over time and will continue to change in the future. From being a society of hunter-gatherers to peasants and farmers, through the industrial revolution to the age of technology, the way in which we work has continually evolved. It is clear that the evolution of work is merely a by-product of the evolution of humanity. It should come as no surprise, then, that this evolution will continue in the future as business, society and the world in which we live are forced to adapt to an ever-changing landscape. What might be surprising, however, is the pace and speed with which this evolution and change will take place – especially as it relates to the workplace. What has led to this expedited evolution of the workplace? Many factors have contributed to shifts in the way we work, but there is one factor in particular that has disproportionately impacted on this evolution – that factor is *technology*. If advances in technology are evolving the way in which work is conducted, how will this impact and shape the future of work and what are the implications for the employees and organizations that will be affected by these changes? The following sections will take a closer look specifically into how technology might significantly change the way we perform work in the future.

How technology will continue to change the way work is performed in the future

Technology impacting on the way people work is certainly not a new concept. One need look no further than the dawn and subsequent decline of the industrial revolution to see the historical impact that technology has had on the workplace. In fact, more than 50 years ago, American President Lyndon B Johnson commissioned a comprehensive study into the potential impact that technology could have on the workplace. As was alluded to earlier, one of the biggest differences between now and the past has been the speed at which that change has taken place. Another difference is that, in the past, technological advances led to the creation of more jobs. These jobs were created because of the need to have individuals who could operate the new technology that had been developed. In this new wave of technological advancement, new jobs are not being created at the same pace as they were in the past. Artificial intelligence has advanced to such a degree that it can take the place of the employees that were once required to operate the new technology. In other words, we are now at a point in time where the new technology that has been developed can operate autonomously – at least more than it could historically.

Because the pace of technological advancement has accelerated significantly in recent years, one of the biggest uncertainties regarding how the impact of technology will affect the workplace centres around the timeline for when these changes will begin to materialize and actually impact on society, the labour market and the way work is performed in the organization. Before exploring this challenge in more detail, however, more context should be provided regarding what is specifically meant by technological advances in the way work is or will be performed in the future.

At its core, technological advances in the workplace (and the workforce) refer to jobs and tasks that were once or are currently carried out by people that can now be automated and hence performed by machines. The reason why this is possible now where it was not in the past is because of the massive advances in the computational efficiency of computers. This increase in computing power has provided scientists and researchers with the horse power required to develop powerful algorithms that enable the computers to effectively teach themselves. When the terms 'machine learning' or 'artificial intelligence' are used, this is to what they refer. As it relates to automation, this increase in computational power coupled with these sophisticated algorithms have led to a reality where machines can be trained to perform certain tasks that were once thought impossible. Furthermore, many of the actions these machines can perform are tasks that usually would have been carried out by humans, but now can be completed more efficiently, with fewer errors and more cost-effectively, by these machines than those people ever could have achieved on their own. It should come as no surprise that many organizations see massive opportunities to reduce costs while improving productivity and efficiency by utilising the automation that these machines now can provide. All of these confounding factors have led to a new age of automation in the workplace that has the potential to dramatically alter the way work is conducted in the future.

Knowing what we now know about the possible disruption that automation might have in the workplace, the question becomes how profound will this disruption be and when will employees, organizations and society start to feel the effects of these technological advances? Before answering this question, it is necessary to take a closer look at the type of jobs and work that might feel the impact of these advances in technology and automation. In January 2017, the

McKinsey Global Institute published the results of a comprehensive two-year study on the potential disruption that advances in technology might have on the workplace, the workforce and society as a whole. One of the most notable findings from this report relating to how automation might impact on specific jobs and occupations is that, over the next 10–50 years, there will probably only be about 5 per cent of total occupations around the world that are made redundant through automation (Manyika *et al*, 2017). That said, where the impact will be felt more profoundly, however, is on the specific tasks involved in the day-to-day activities of many of the jobs and occupations currently in existence. The study revealed that, if work is broken down on a task-by-task basis, 60 per cent of all occupations will have at least 30 per cent of all tasks currently performed by humans performed by machines in the future (Manyika *et al*, 2017). Regarding activities that face a greater probability of being automated, the study revealed that, not surprisingly, tasks that are more physical or routine in nature and tasks involving data collection will be the activities that will face the greatest risk of being made redundant by machines. This statistic is particularly relevant in developing countries like the United States and the United Kingdom where, in the case of the United States, occupations requiring these tasks make up 51 per cent of all the productivity created in the economy. Moreover, this equates to a staggering US $2.7 trillion in annual wages which can be accounted for by these activities (Manyika *et al*, 2017).

There is clear evidence that automation due to advances in machine learning and artificial intelligence will have a massive impact on the workforce, the workplace and society in general, but when will we start to see the results of this impact take place? The short answer is that the advances in these technologies are already starting to have a notable impact on certain sectors, industries and organizations around the world. For example, based on statistics from the US Bureau of Labor statistics, an estimated five million factory-related jobs have disappeared since 2000 (Long, 2016). Many of these jobs have disappeared due to advances in technology and automation. In more recent years, however, the loss of jobs due to technology and automation spans further than just factory jobs; for example:

- In January 2017, Infosys Inc, an Indian IT services company, laid off 9,000 workers due to automation from machine learning (Phadnis and Ranjani, 2017).

- In March 2017, BlackRock Inc, the world's largest money management firm, announced that 13 per cent of its portfolio managers would be laid off in favour of machine learning algorithms that had been proven to be more accurate and profitable in picking stocks than the company's portfolio managers (Templeton, 2017).

- In May 2016, Foxconn, a Chinese manufacturing firm that acts as one of Apple's largest suppliers, announced that 60,000 workers or 90 per cent of its workforce would be laid off in favour of an automated workforce (Wakefield, 2016).

- In November 2016, McDonald's announced that, in the coming years in the United States, every one of its 14,000 restaurants nationwide would have some level of cashiers replaced by automated touch-screen kiosks (Rensi, 2016).

With more context provided regarding how pervasive the impact of technology and automation will be on the workforce, workplace and society, the question of when this impact will begin to materialize now can be addressed. Answering this question depends on several factors. The McKinsey report, in fact, outlines five distinct themes that have the potential to affect the timeline for when some of the aforementioned changes will take place (see Figure 13.1).

Degree of difficulty to develop the technology

The first theme relates to the technical feasibility required to automate some of the tasks that could be within the scope for automation. What this refers to is whether or not the technology required for the automation is already developed and, if it is not, how long and complicated the development process for that technology might be. In other words, if the technology ends up being more challenging to develop, implement and integrate than originally thought, it could push the timeline out regarding the impact it might have on the jobs and tasks it is designed to replace.

Figure 13.1 Factors that could affect the timeline for workforce automation due to new technology

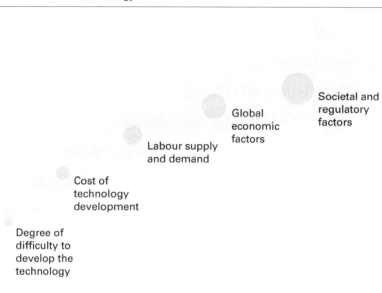

Cost of technology development

Another area for consideration when attempting to assess a timeline for the impact of automation is the cost of developing and adopting the new technologies in question. If the technology ends up being more cost-prohibitive than was initially thought, it could delay the development and adoption of that technology in automating tasks.

Labour supply and demand

The supply of and demand for skills across the globe is another factor that could potentially impact on progress towards automation. The equilibrium between the supply of and demand for skills affects the cost of those skills, which in turn affects the degree to which there will be an economic benefit from automation rather than having employees perform the tasks. If the expense of the skills in the labour market is cheaper than it would cost to develop, implement and adopt new technology to automate those skills, it makes sense, economically speaking, for companies to pursue this option. If this ends up being the scenario that plays out, it will delay the time that it takes for automation to be adopted.

Global economic factors

Another factor that could impact on the timeline of which automation has an impact relates to broader global economic factors. If unforeseen economic events end up influencing the economic health of countries and organizations within those countries, it could delay the development and implementation of the technologies required for automation. This would consequently delay the timeline for these technologies to start to affect society and the workplace.

Societal and regulatory factors

Finally, there are societal and regulatory factors that inevitably will play a role in the timeline for which technological advancements in automation become mainstream enough to impact on the way employees, companies and societies perform their work. As regulatory and societal factors begin to play a larger role in the discussions concerning how automation and the future of work stand to impact on society, this topic will become more important. Much consideration will have to go into addressing questions and concerns regarding training, taxes and unemployment as regulators, lawmakers and industry leaders weigh up the pros and cons that technological advances in automation will have on the wellbeing of society, industry and business as a whole.

Understanding the role of SWP in the future of work

There is no question that advances in technology are creating workplaces around the world where many of the tasks and responsibilities traditionally performed by humans soon will be replaced by machines – if machines have not already replaced them. The change and transformation required to both minimize the disruption to employees working in roles that will be impacted by new technologies and automation, while also maximizing the potential productivity gains from the new technologies being implemented, will be significant. Due to the high level of planning that will be required to make the transition to workforce automation as smooth as possible, the SWP function is uniquely positioned with the skills and capabilities to provide significant guidance to the organization through this transition.

Depending on the industry and business, for many organizations, the concept of these new technologies still may be an abstract theory. For these organizations, the notion of machine learning, artificial intelligence and automation is either not on their radar, or seems like something that will happen too far in the future to start thinking about or planning for today. What many organizational leaders may not be aware of, though, is how soon these technologies could potentially begin to impact on their organizations. It is for this reason that part of the role of the SWP function should be to provide organizational leaders with insights into *how*, *where* and *when* automation and other advances in technology could impact on their workforces and broader organizations for that matter. These three categories also provide a framework for the SWP practitioner to think through regarding the questions and answers that should be discussed with leaders in the foundational phase of planning and designing a workforce of the future that includes automation and new technologies.

How automation and new technologies will impact on the future workforce

This section looks at how disruptive an impact the adoption and implementation of automation and new technologies might have on the workforce. The organization needs to ensure that the right policies and programmes are in place to help alleviate the possibility of that disruption if and when this automation becomes a reality for the organization. Questions to think through include:

- Will automation create new jobs or render current jobs redundant?

- Will automation and new technology lead to a need for more training?

- Are the organization's current training and development programmes mature enough to handle the level of training that might be required to adapt to the new technologies?

- What is the demographic profile of the organization's current workforce? Are they technical? Are they younger or more mature?
- If new technical skills will be required, is the organization located in a region or area that has a healthy supply of technical talent to support that demand?
- If automation and new technologies lead to job losses, what type of support structure is in place for employees whose jobs might become redundant?
- For employees who end up losing their jobs, are there opportunities for new roles in the organization? If so, how can the organization ensure it optimally matches the right candidates with the right jobs?

Where in the organization the impact of automation and new technologies will be most profound

This section involves assessing the jobs and tasks across the organization to try and understand which of those jobs and tasks might be more likely to be affected by new technologies and automation. There are two key questions to be answered here. First, which jobs are most likely to be impacted by automation and new technology? A good starting point for answering this question is to look across all the roles in the organization and rate them based on the probability that the entire role could be automated. As an example, a cashier at a fast-food restaurant has a much greater probability of having their job made redundant than a fashion designer for a clothing manufacturer. Second, and more importantly than the specific jobs that might be replaceable through automation, what is the percentage of tasks within each job that have the potential to be replaced by automation? In this exercise the SWP practitioner should go through each job or role in the organization and evaluate each task against the probability of that task potentially becoming automated. A good rule of thumb for this evaluation is to assume that routine tasks of a physical nature along with data-processing tasks have a greater likelihood of being automated, whereas tasks that require higher-level cognitive reasoning and logic have a lesser likelihood of being automated (at least in the short term). These two activities should be performed at

Figure 13.2 Example of assessing the probability of a job or task being automated in the future

Job	Probability of automation
A	0.2
B	0.6
C	0.3
D	0.8
E	0.1
F	0.4

Task	Probability of automation
A	0.1
B	0.9
C	0.45
D	0.02
E	0.7
F	0.3

the site, country and regional level to gain a sense of which locations might be more prone to be affected by automation than others (see Figure 13.2).

When the organization potentially could feel the effects of automation and new technologies

This section involves evaluating the timeline for feasible implementation of new technologies and automation in the workforce against the five criteria that could accelerate or decelerate automation in accordance with what was discussed earlier in the chapter. Questions to consider include:

- Is the technology required for automation already a reality? Are competitors or comparable industries already utilizing the technology? If not, how long might it take to develop this technology?

- How expensive is the technology to develop or implement? If the technology is expensive to develop and implement, how long would it take, if ever, for the technology to be priced at a point where it might be economically feasible to develop or implement?

- What is the cost of labour for the organization regarding the roles that might be in scope for automation? Is the cost of this labour expensive or cheap? If the labour is cheap, would the automation be cheaper than the labour already in place? If not, is the cost of labour rising or will the cost of the technology become more competitive in coming years?

- What does the current and future economic health look like for the organization and industry in which the organization competes? Is the health of the organization and industry such that it would make sense to invest in new automation technologies?

- Does the organization compete in an industry where political, social or regulatory factors could impede the progress of automation? Are these factors improving or getting worse?

Summary of chapter objectives

How the landscape of work is changing

The way that work is performed is in a constant state of flux. This is not a new concept, but rather one that has been evolving since man has walked the planet. What is changing, however, is the rate and speed of the evolution in the way work is being performed. There are two notable factors that are contributing to this exponential rate of change in the landscape of work. The first factor is the gig economy (discussed in Chapter 9), which has led to an increase in the number of freelancers in the job market (workers such as Uber drivers). The impact of the rise in popularity of working as a freelancer has begun to transform the labour market into a market of on-demand skills and jobs. The second factor is technology and automation, which are making many of the jobs and tasks previously performed by humans redundant.

The role of technology in the changing landscape of work

As was alluded to in the last section, technology is a huge factor that is shaping how work is changing today and will change in the future. What this really means is that, due to advances in machine learning and artificial intelligence, machines are now able to perform many of the tasks that were once performed by people. It should be noted that automation in the future probably will not replace entire jobs, but will replace a certain percentage of tasks involved in the day-to-day activities of those jobs. Jobs that require data entry and more repetitive physical tasks are at higher risk of automation than jobs that require more logic and cognitive reasoning. An example of a job that is at high risk of being replaced by automation is a cashier at a fast-food restaurant or a lower-level data-entry clerk at an accounting firm.

The role of SWP in the future of work

Depending on the industry and business, for many organizations, the concept of these new technologies still may be an abstract theory. For these organizations, the notion of machine learning, artificial intelligence and automation is either not on their radar, or seems like something that will happen too far in the future to start thinking about or planning for today. What many organizational leaders may not be aware of, though, is how soon these technologies potentially could begin to impact on their organizations. It is for this reason that part of the role of the SWP function should be to provide organizational leaders with insights into how, where and when automation and other advances in technology could impact on their workforces and broader organizations for that matter. These three categories also provide a framework for the SWP practitioner to think through regarding the questions and answers that should be discussed with leaders in the foundational phase of planning and designing a workforce of the future that accounts for automation and new technologies.

Bringing it all together 14

Overview

The final chapter in this book will provide the SWP practitioner and any other stakeholder involved or interested in the SWP process with a summary guide on how to take the book's key learnings and incorporate them into a robust and flexible Strategic Workforce Plan. It will provide commentary on the steps the SWP practitioner should take to ensure the Strategic Workforce Plan accounts for the unique operating environment and needs of the organization, external factors and other workforce-related issues that could affect it, in order to add value and improve organizational performance.

Creating the vision for the SWP function

Chapter 11 of this book provided a comprehensive overview of considerations regarding the creation of a vision for the Strategic Workforce Plan. For the organization to develop an effective Strategic Workforce Plan, there first must be considerable thought put into the purpose or vision of what both the SWP function or team and the Strategic Workforce Plan itself will encompass. Creating a vision is important because it sets the tone and direction for the actions and milestones the organization needs to accomplish in order to deliver on the function's broader objectives. Without a solid vision in place, the SWP function is effectively walking in the dark. Lack of a solid vision is one of the primary reasons why many SWP teams never live up to their full potential. Without that vision, it becomes difficult for the organization to know the specific details it should address when putting the initial building blocks in place to create a Strategic Workforce Plan that delivers the intended value. Creating a vision for the success of an SWP function is not an activity the organization should take lightly, nor is it an activity that should be completed in haste. Developing a vision for the SWP function involves three key areas:

1 thinking through how the SWP function will contribute to the success of the company's broader mission;

2 narrowing in on the focus of the vision;

3 socialization and validation of the vision.

Building an SWP team

Chapter 11 also provided context on the skills and team composition that the SWP function should comprise. Depending upon the size of the organization and the vision for the SWP function, the make-up of this team can be anywhere from a single individual to a fully-fledged function encompassing dozens of team members. Regardless of whether the SWP function is small or large, there are some key factors the organization should think about before creating this team. Thinking through the skills, competencies, experience and education levels of the SWP function is crucial. Ultimately, it will be the individuals on this team that will be performing the necessary actions – from a day-to-day perspective – required to execute and deliver on the SWP vision.

As discussed earlier in the book, a useful framework to leverage when creating the talent profiles of the SWP team is to use the SWP and analytics maturity curve. These are useful in this context because the specific skills that leaders should be thinking about regarding the vision alignment and level of impact are typically analytical. The earlier example of requiring employees to have the ability to create optimization models provides a good illustration of this. Depending upon the end goal for the SWP function, the SWP team's composition should align with the skills that are required at each stage of this curve. The following section provides a reminder of the key skills, competencies and education required at each stage of this maturity curve.

Basic reporting

Basic reporting is the foundational phase of the Strategic Workforce Plan and workforce analytics maturity curve. In this phase, organizations typically are pulling basic reports from an HRIS data warehouse. The structure of these reports is generally raw data in the form of an Excel spreadsheet. Basic reporting is also an essential aspect of SWP because the SWP function will rely heavily on raw data and reports as a starting point for many of the workforce-related analyses that will be conducted. The skills required are:

- SQL;
- Excel;
- database administration.

Dashboarding and metrics reporting

This stage can be characterized by the creation of pivot tables, dashboards and more robust reporting. At this part of the maturity curve, the objective goes from simply pulling basic reports to transforming and manipulating the data and content of those reports into charts, tables and visualizations that provide more intuitive insight into the different dimensions of the workforce. A large component of SWP involves measuring and tracking the health and progress of the organization's workforce against the workforce strategy and Strategic Workforce Plan that the SWP function has created. Measuring and tracking is accomplished through dashboards and metrics reporting. The skills required are:

- SQL;
- Excel;
- database administration;
- data visualization;
- business acumen;
- consulting;
- presentation skills.

Descriptive analytics

As opposed to the first two stages of the maturity curve that dealt with creating basic reports and dashboards from HRIS systems data, the descriptive insights stage is more focused on analysing the underlying data. At this stage, the organization begins to place a greater emphasis on determining and analysing the root causes of and factors that may be contributing to workforce-related events or trends that are impacting on the business. Because SWP involves assessing the current state of the workforce against a desired future state, it is important for the SWP function to be able to understand events that are happening in the current workforce that could impact on the success of the future workforce. The skills required are:

- SQL;
- Excel;
- database administration;
- data visualization;
- business acumen;
- consulting;
- presentation skills;
- statistics;
- data curiosity.

Predictive insights

The final stage of the SWP and workforce analytics maturity curve jumps from descriptive analytics, where the analyst is using statistical techniques to try and understand why a workforce-related event happened, to prescriptive analytics, where the analyst is now attempting to predict what will occur in the future. For the SWP function, this is the stage of the Strategic Workforce Plan and workforce analytics maturity curve that might be the most important because, at the most fundamental level, SWP seeks to understand what, if any, gaps exist between the current state of an organization's workforce and some desired future state. For the SWP function to be able to assess this gap requires predicting potential future scenarios. For the SWP function to be able to predict these scenarios requires the function to have an aptitude for predictive analytics. The skills required are:

- SQL;
- Excel;
- database administration;
- data visualization;
- business acumen;
- consulting;
- presentation skills;
- statistics;
- data curiosity;
- machine learning;
- forecasting.

Defining the organization's SWP process

In a similar way to having a clear understanding and definition of what the organization's SWP vision will look like, there is an equally important demand to have clearly defined processes and procedures in place regarding how the Strategic Workforce Plan will be incorporated into the organization's broader operations. This is another component of building an effective SWP function that should be in place in the early stages of building out the team. As was discussed earlier in the book, building out effective systems, processes and procedures for the SWP function requires having a plan in place for how the company will organize and operationalize the day-to-day activities on which the SWP team will work. This is another foundational aspect of building an effective and efficient SWP function. Like the other foundational components, developing a systems, process and scalability plan involves some detailed upfront thought and collaboration from the organization's leaders. The primary questions these leaders should be asking regarding these processes and systems are:

1 *Intake and outtake process:* How can the function guarantee that the stakeholders requiring information have a platform and system in place to ask for that information or data? Also, how can the function ensure that the stakeholders requesting information get the information they are looking for in a timely manner, in the format they want and with enough context to feel comfortable sharing the information with other leaders and cross-functional partners in the organization?

2 *Scaling and growth:* How does the organization scale and grow the above intake and outtake process?

3 *Prioritization:* How do the SWP team members prioritize the projects and analyses on which they work?

4 *Corporate strategy planning:* How does the organization incorporate SWP into the ongoing corporate planning process?

Incorporating data and technology into the SWP process

The final foundational component that should be considered in the design of an SWP function is the role that data and technology will play in providing workforce insights to the organization. Not thinking through the data and technology component of the SWP process is another trap that many organizations fall into in the early stages of the SWP journey. The danger of not thinking through this component in the initial stages of building out an SWP function risks running into data quality issues with no technology in place to scale the insights that the function hopes to provide to the organization.

Data

On several occasions, this book has highlighted the importance of ensuring the data that are being used to analyse internal and external workforce-related factors are reliable, consistent and error-free. For this reason, it is imperative that the organization goes through two key data-related activities before formally implementing an SWP function across the organization. The first of these activities is a *data quality assessment*. A data quality assessment is just the activity of going through all of the data tables in the organization's HRIS system to ensure the data are accurate, relevant and not missing any observations. The second activity is an *inventory analysis* of what data the organization currently possesses. A data inventory analysis is the exercise of doing an 'inventory check' of all the data in the organization's HRIS data warehouse. All of the data fields that are checked in this analysis should be recorded and catalogued for future reference.

Technology

The importance of technology in the SWP process is another key theme that has been discussed throughout the book. Technology in the context of scaling and growing an SWP function refers to the tools that will be used to analyse and visualize data, creating self-service capabilities for key stakeholders and the platform on which the insights will be delivered to the organization. The key factors that should be assessed for each of the possible technology solutions include:

- cost of the technology;
- scalability of the technology;
- usability of the technology;
- sophistication level of the technology;
- skills required to use the technology.

Developing a baseline understanding of the composition of the workforce

Once the SWP mission has been developed, a team structure is in place, the processes and systems required to support the SWP process have been established and the technology required to scale, grow and maximize the impact of the SWP function have been agreed upon, it is time to develop a Strategic Workforce Plan. The level of detail that goes into the Strategic Workforce Plan's initial baseline data set depends on how ambitious and aggressive the organization's vision and goals for its plan are. At a minimum, however, the SWP function should go through the process of analysing, organizing and categorizing the following data fields (see Figure 14.1):

- *Current FTE headcount:* The total number of FTEs that work for the organization.

- *Current contractor/contingent worker headcount:* The total number of contractors and contingent workers that work in the organization.

- *Historical FTE headcount growth:* A historical time-series trend that tracks FTE headcount.

- *Historical contractor/contingent worker headcount growth:* A historical time-series trend that tracks contractor and contingent worker headcount.

- *Current total attrition:* The total number of FTEs that have left the organization in the previous 12 months divided by the average FTE headcount for that period.

- *Current regrettable attrition:* The total number of regrettable FTEs (employees the organization regrets losing) that have left the organization in the previous 12 months divided by the average FTE headcount for that period.

- *Current non-regrettable attrition:* The total number of non-regrettable FTEs (employees the organization does not regret losing) that have left the organization in the previous 12 months divided by the average FTE headcount for that period.

- *Historical total attrition:* The same methodology as for current attrition, but over a longer time period of three to five years.

- *Historical regrettable attrition:* The same methodology as for current attrition, but over a longer time period of three to five years.

- *Historical non-regrettable attrition:* The same methodology as for current attrition, but over a longer time period of three to five years.

Figure 14.1 Variables to include in the baseline numbers for a Strategic Workforce Plan

Baseline factor	Location	Country	Region	Business unit	Function	Department	Team	Job level
FTE headcount								
Contractor/contingent worker headcount								
Historical headcount growth								
Contractor/contingent worker headcount growth								
Total attrition								
Regrettable attrition								
Non–regrettable attrition								
Historical total attrition								
Historical non-regrettable attrition								
Historical regrettable attrition								
Internal transfers								
Historical internal transfers								
Promotion distribution								
Tenure distribution								
Age distribution								
Performance evaluation distribution								

- *Internal transfers:* Employees who have transferred to new roles within the organization over the current 12-month period.

- *Historical internal transfers:* Employees who have transferred to new roles within the organization over a historical three to five-year period.

- *Promotion distribution:* Current distribution of promotions by factors such as function and location.

- *Tenure distribution:* Distribution of the total workforce by the length of time employees have been with the organization.

- *Age distribution:* Distribution of the total workforce by the current age of employees.

- *Performance evaluation distribution:* Distribution of performance evaluations based on rating categories currently and over time.

This list is not fully comprehensive, but does include fields that should be considered minimum requirements in developing a holistic Strategic Workforce Plan. It is also worth noting that the SWP practitioner should ensure that the legal and compliance team has been given the opportunity to review some of the more sensitive data fields, such as age and performance evaluation. This is mainly to ensure compliance with any governmental or organizational regulations regarding the analysis of the data, because it is essential not to break any rules or put the organization at any legal risk.

Workforce segmentation

With the baseline data in place for the Strategic Workforce Plan, attention should be turned to segmenting the workforce into critical workforce segments. While this is not an activity that should be considered mandatory, it is recommended because it provides leaders with a framework for prioritizing aspects of the workforce that are driving a disproportionate amount of value or risk. Regarding workforce segmentation, the ultimate goal should be to divide the workforce into segments that drive a disproportionate amount of value relative to the other segments. As was discussed in Chapter 5, there tend to be three key features that are synonymous with critical workforce segments and these are:

1 a segment of the workforce where the skills make-up of that segment tends to be in high demand or low supply relative to the skills in other segments of the organization;

2 a segment of the workforce that has a disproportionate amount of impact on the organization's value chain;

3 a segment of the workforce that drives a disproportionate number of positive business outcomes.

Using these three factors as a starting point and leveraging some of the activities discussed in Chapter 5, the SWP practitioner should be able to identify the workforce segments that are most critical, relevant and practical for their organization's unique operating environment.

Developing workforce supply and demand projections

With the baseline workforce data in place and the critical workforce segments established, the next step in developing a Strategic Workforce Plan is to develop a forecast or a 'future state' for internal supply of and demand for talent. There are four components to developing these projections, as discussed in Chapters 3 and 4.

Developing an attrition model that will forecast how the supply of internal talent will dwindle over time due to attrition

Creating an attrition forecast provides the SWP practitioner, along with HR and business leaders, with insights into how much hiring will be required, if hiring is actually required, to backfill the roles that were left vacant due to that attrition. The skills, experience and education of the employees that are hired from attrition backfill should align with the organization's broader, forward-looking, corporate strategy. It is important to note that, because strategic objectives in organizations flex with the dynamic nature of the external business environment in which the companies operate, the employees hired as backfill may have significantly different profiles than their predecessors. Understanding and informing business leaders on what these new profiles could and should look like comprises a key part of the SWP process.

Providing insights and forecasts on what the supply of talent will look like in the external labour market in the future

Many organizations compete on talent and technical skills, and even for those that do not, but still require more generic skills and jobs to complete day-to-day activities, it is important to understand what the availability or supply of these skills and roles will look like in the future. To do this requires an understanding of the variables that impact on talent supply and how changes and trends in those variables might impact on the future supply of talent. Some of these factors include things such as new entrants into the labour market through university, college and trade-school graduations, shifts in career paths and exits from the labour market due to retirement.

Providing forecasts of future demand for skills, experience and education based on key business drivers in the organization

In addition to having an understanding of how the supply of the organization's talent will change over time, it is equally important to understand what the demand for that talent will be. Understanding the future demand for skills, experience and education that the organization will require to execute on its corporate strategy involves first understanding the business drivers that impact on this demand. The SWP practitioner should partner closely with business and HR leaders to develop a list of demand drivers. Once potential demand drivers have been identified, the SWP practitioner should use a combination of advanced statistical techniques, practical experience and common sense to ensure that the relationships between these business drivers and the future demand for the organization's skills, experience and education are real. Once the relationships between business drivers and employee demand have been established, forecasts then should be developed based on the organization's strategy and projections for those business drivers. Doing this will provide the SWP practitioner with tangible numbers regarding the future growth or retraction of headcount and the accompanying skills, experience and education to include in the Strategic Workforce Plan.

Providing insights into and forecasts of what the future demand for talent will look like in the external labour market in the future

Factoring external workforce demand into a Strategic Workforce Plan is critical because it is the starting point for understanding how much competition there is for the skills and jobs around the world or in the local region. Accurately assessing the external demand for these skills and jobs is crucial in order to answer questions such as the following:

- Is demand for the organization's critical expertise and jobs increasing, decreasing or remaining the same in the external labour market?

- Is the demand for these skills concentrated in a particular industry or are changes in demand being felt across the entire sector?

- Are there locations where demand is higher or is demand steady across the globe?

- Is there a trend for more or less demand for these skills and jobs in the external labour market?

- Is increased demand driving up the cost of labour for these skills and jobs?

- Are there new technologies that have the potential to impact on future demand?

- Are there any trends in university graduation rates for specific degree programmes that can be leading indicators of changes in workforce demand?

Developing a workforce strategy

With critical workforce segments established and supply and demand projections in place, it is now time to analyse the outputs of these analyses and compare them to the organization's long-term corporate objectives to establish a workforce strategy that ultimately will become the backbone and guiding principle for the creation of the Strategic Workforce Plan. As was discussed in Chapter 2, a workforce strategy is the starting point for developing a Strategic Workforce Plan and is built from the outputs of the previous steps outlined in this chapter. When done properly, a workforce strategy should be a component of the broader corporate strategy. One of the keys to developing a reliable workforce strategy is ensuring the organization's key performance indicators, such as number of products manufactured or number of platform users or new products developed, are in sync with workforce-related outcomes such as the right skills to develop those new products. Ensuring the existence of a stable relationship between the two provides the SWP practitioner with a method for quantifying and optimizing future workforce requirements based on the strategic direction of the company.

Aligning the workforce strategy with the corporate strategy begins with understanding the corporate strategy. Key elements of most corporate strategies include:

- long-term vision of the company;
- scope of activities required to achieve the long-term vision;
- competitive positioning of the company *vis-à-vis* competitors;
- the organization's resources, whether in terms of employees or equipment;
- culture of the organization.

In addition to understanding the corporate strategy, it is important to understand internal and external factors that have the potential to impact on the workforce strategy. Key considerations that have the ability to affect a workforce strategy include:

- the labour market;
- current technology;

- future technology;
- corporate strategy decisions.

Developing workforce strategies and Strategic Workforce Plans in tandem with the organization's corporate strategy creates significantly more value for the organization than creating these plans and strategies in silos. Creating workforce strategies in silos is one of the reasons that, historically, the HR function has not been thought of as a partner in creating the same level of value throughout the enterprise as more traditional functions like marketing and R&D. It is also for this reason that many organizations have missed out on the opportunity to realize the benefits and added value that HR has the potential to bring to corporate strategy discussions.

Additional considerations

Regarding the development of the final Strategic Workforce Plan, there are a few other factors that have been discussed in this book that, depending on the organization's vision for the SWP function, should be considered and factored into the final plan. These other topics include:

- total cost of the workforce (TCOW);
- site-selection and location strategy;
- contractors and contingent workforce strategy;
- change management;
- future of work.

Total cost of the workforce (TCOW)

One important factor that should be considered when developing a workforce strategy and Strategic Workforce Plan is the cost of that strategy. Chapter 6 discussed why the SWP practitioner should think of costs associated with workforce or HR programmes as constraints that the organization needs to consider in order to reach an 'optimal' workforce state. What this means is that, when the final Strategic Workforce Plan is in place, there should be costs associated with all the forecasts and scenarios that account for factors such as headcount growth or retraction, location planning, training and development payroll and other workforce-related programmes. Assigning costs to all of these factors will give the SWP practitioner a baseline for assessing a metric known as the TCOW. The benefit of establishing the TCOW is that, when this metric is in place, the company can then measure the performance of its workforce strategy by the costs associated with managing and growing the workforce. When workforce-related costs are growing higher than productivity and efficiency gains, it is a sign that the workforce strategy the organization is pursuing is not optimal. On the flip side, when costs are shrinking relative to the productivity, performance and efficiency of its workforce, the organization is executing well on its Strategic Workforce Plan. One of the main advantages of including costs in a Strategic Workforce Plan is that it gives the SWP practitioner the ability to work with business and HR leaders to create scenarios that model out different cost-benefit structures for workforce-related decisions.

Site-selection and location strategy

Chapter 8 discussed the importance of an organization thinking strategically about how it approaches site-selection and location strategies. The importance of thinking about these strategies is magnified when the impact that locations potentially can have on the organization's workforce is factored in. The ability to attract, retain and develop key talent invariably will be a factor that plays a role in a particular location's success or failure within the organization's broader corporate strategy. SWP can and should play a significant part in helping the organization's business leaders think through how the talent and workforce associated with a particular location can impact on that location's ability to be successful within the company's longer-term strategic objectives. More specifically, SWP can help to inform location decisions by providing insight into a variety of factors. A few of these factors include:

- talent supply and availability in the location's market;
- FTE and contingent employee growth forecasts for the location;
- competitor talent intelligence in the location space planning optimization for positive employee experience at the location;
- current and future state talent scenario analysis;
- quality of life and cost of living information for the location.

Contractors and contingent workforce strategy

Chapter 9 discussed the importance of accounting for contingent workers and contractors in the SWP process. Incorporation into the organization's workforce strategy and finalized Strategic Workforce Plan involves taking the methodology and steps outlined above and layering the contingent workforce and contractors into that plan. Effectively, the SWP practitioner should treat contingent workers and contractors as another element of the workforce that needs to be analysed and accounted for in the same way as the FTE workforce.

Change management

Introducing SWP as a new business process can involve a significant amount of change to an organization. With change typically comes a natural human response to resist that change. Therefore, it is important to ensure that a robust change-management plan has been developed in conjunction with the implementation of a new SWP function and process. Chapter 12 outlined the following activities as being crucial in the development of a good SWP change-management plan:

- describing the purpose of the change;
- describing the specifics of the change;
- outlining the change-management framework to be used;
- describing the actions required to adopt the change;
- outlining the specifics of how the change-management strategy will be implemented;
- developing an action plan for the implementation of the change-management strategy;

- developing a communications plan to be used in conjunction with the change-management plan;
- developing a training plan to be used in conjunction with the change-management plan;
- developing a plan of how the organization will overcome resistance to the new change.

Future of work

The final consideration in the development of a robust Strategic Workforce Plan is how the future of technology and the way work is performed potentially could impact on the workforce. Depending on the industry and business, for many organizations, the concept of these technologies that could revolutionize the way work is performed is nothing more than an abstract theory. For these organizations, the notion of machine learning, artificial intelligence and automation is either not on their radar, or seems like something that will happen too far in the future to start thinking about or planning for today. What many organizational leaders may not be aware of, though, is how soon these technologies potentially could begin to impact on their organizations. So, part of the role of the SWP function should be to provide organizational leaders with insight into *how*, *where* and *when* automation and other advances in technology could impact on their workforces and broader organizations for that matter. These three categories also provide a framework for the SWP practitioner to think through regarding the questions and answers that should be discussed with leaders in the foundational phase of planning and designing a workforce of the future that accounts for automation and new technologies.

1 How will automation and new technologies impact on the future workforce?

2 Where in the organization will the impact of automation and new technologies be most profound?

3 When could the organization potentially feel the effects of automation and new technologies?

Summary

The intention of this book is to provide SWP practitioners, individuals and organizations new to SWP, along with HR and business leaders, insight into how SWP can provide value and increase organizational efficiencies. The book outlines practical strategies and examples of how, when and where SWP can be used, providing SWP stakeholders with a guide on different aspects of SWP and factors both internally and externally that have the potential to impact on the SWP process. Organizations that choose to utilize and incorporate SWP as part of their ongoing business processes have the potential to bridge a significant gap that often exists between an organization's corporate strategy and the development and optimization of its workforce. When done properly, one can think of the SWP function as the engineer that builds this bridge. The end goal and reward for a properly constructed bridge is a high-functioning workforce that adds value and supports the company in achieving its broader mission and corporate objectives. To that end, my intention is for this book to be considered as a blueprint for the ongoing construction efforts in the building of this bridge. I wish everyone involved in the SWP process the best of luck and success in their endeavours to build the perfect SWP bridge. I sincerely appreciate you taking the time to read this book and hope you have enjoyed it and learned some valuable, practical and real-world lessons that can add value to you and your respective organizations.

REFERENCES

Chapter 1

Bechet, T P (2008) *Strategic Staffing: A Comprehensive System for Effective Workforce Planning*, AMACOM, Division of American Management Association, New York

Lewin, K (2008) Quasi-stationary social equilibria and the problem of permanent change, in *Organization Change: A Comprehensive Reader*, ed W W Burke, D G Lake and J Waymire Paine, pp 73–77, Jossey-Bass, San Francisco

Noe, R A *et al* (2003) *Gaining a Competitive Advantage*, McGraw-Hill/Irwin, New York

Wood, R, Bandura, A and Bailey, T (1990) Mechanisms governing organizational performance in complex decision-making environments, *Organizational Behavior and Human Decision Processes*, **46** (2), pp 181–201

Chapter 2

Ansoff, H I and McDonnell, E J (1988) *The New Corporate Strategy*, John Wiley & Sons Inc, Hoboken, NJ

Gubman, E (1998) *The Talent Solution: Aligning Strategy and People to Achieve Extraordinary Results*, McGraw Hill Professional, New York

Huselid, M A, Becker, B E and Beatty, R W (2005) *The Workforce Scorecard: Managing Human Capital to Execute Strategy*, Harvard Business Review Press, Boston

Needle, D (2010) *Business in Context: An Introduction to Business and Its Environment*, Cengage Learning (EMEA) Ltd, Andover, Hampshire

Parmenter, D (2015) *Key Performance Indicators: Developing, Implementing, and Using Winning KPIs*, John Wiley & Sons, Oxford

Chapter 3

Hamermesh, D S (1996) *Labor Demand*, Princeton University Press, N J

Merrett, A J and Sykes, A (1973) *The Finance and Analysis of Capital Projects*, John Wiley & Sons, Oxford

Chapter 4

Box, G E *et al* (2015) *Time Series Analysis: Forecasting and Control*, John Wiley & Sons, Oxford

Cascio, W F and Aguinis, H (2005) *Applied Psychology in Human Resource Management*, Pearson Education Inc, Upper Saddle River, NJ

Duffy, J (2001) The tools and technologies needed for knowledge management, *Information Management*, 35 (1), p 64

Gardner, E S (1985) Exponential smoothing: The state of the art, *Journal of Forecasting*, 4 (1), pp 1–28

Hamilton, J D (1994) *Time Series Analysis*, Vol 2, Princeton University Press, NJ

Koch, M J and McGrath, R G (1996) Improving labor productivity: Human resource management policies do matter, *Strategic Management Journal*, 17 (5), pp 335–54

Rasool, F and Botha, C J (2011) The nature, extent and effect of skills shortages on skills migration in South Africa, *SA Journal of Human Resource Management*, 9 (1), pp 1–12

Reh, F J (2005) Pareto's principle – The 80-20 rule, *Business Credit-New York Then Columbia MD*, 107 (7), p 76

Chapter 5

Lavelle, J (2007) On workforce architecture, employment relationships and lifecycles: Expanding the purview of workforce planning & management, *Public Personnel Management*, 36 (4), pp 371–85

Porter, M E (2008) *Competitive Advantage: Creating and Sustaining Superior Performance*, Simon and Schuster, New York

Reh, F J (2005) Pareto's principle – The 80-20 rule, *Business Credit-New York Then Columbia MD*, 107 (7), p 76

Chapter 6

Cascio, W F (1986) *Managing Human Resources*, McGraw-Hill, New York

Kaplan, R S and Cooper, R (1998) *Cost & Effect: Using Integrated Cost Systems to Drive Profitability and Performance*, Harvard Business School Press, Boston

McEachern, W A (2011) *Economics: A Contemporary Introduction*, Cengage South-Western, Mason, O H

Rappaport, A (1986) *Creating Shareholder Value: The New Standard for Business Performance*, Free Press, New York

Chapter 7

Duffy, J (2001) The tools and technologies needed for knowledge management, *Information Management*, 35 (1), p 64

Koch, M J and McGrath, R G (1996) Improving labor productivity: Human resource management policies do matter, *Strategic Management Journal*, 17 (5), pp 335–54

Snell, S A and Dean, J W (1992) Integrated manufacturing and human resource management: A human capital perspective, *Academy of Management Journal*, 35 (3), pp 467–504

Chapter 8

http://www.bankrate.com/calculators/savings/moving-cost-of-living-calculator.aspx

Kawa, L [accessed 17 November 2017] Older Americans Are Retiring in Droves, *Bloomberg* [Online] https://www.bloomberg.com/news/articles/2017-01-06/older-americans-are-retiring-in-droves

Earle, H A (2003) Building a workplace of choice: Using the work environment to attract and retain top talent, *Journal of Facilities Management*, 2 (3), pp 244–57

Kim, J and de Dear, R (2013) Workspace satisfaction: The privacy-communication trade-off in open-plan offices, *Journal of Environmental Psychology*, 36, pp 18–26

Leblebici, D (2012) Impact of workplace quality on employee's productivity: Case study of a bank in Turkey, *Journal of Business Economics and Finance*, 1 (1), pp 38–49

https://www.numbeo.com/cost-of-living/comparison.jsp

Schrantz, K P (2013) Location and competitive strategy in retail: The case of GameStop in Michigan, master's thesis, Western Michigan University, Kalamazoo

http://swz.salary.com/CostOfLivingWizard/LayoutScripts/Coll_Start.aspx

Vischer, J C (2012) *Workspace Strategies: Environment as a Tool for Work*, Springer Science & Business Media, Berlin

Chapter 9

Allan, P (2002) The contingent workforce: Challenges and new directions, *American Business Review*, 20 (2), p 103–10

Mallon, M and Duberley, J (2000) Managers and professionals in the contingent workforce, *Human Resource Management Journal*, 10 (1), pp 33–47

Paychex (2016) [accessed 17 November 2017] Goodbye, 9-5! The Growth of the Freelance Economy [Online] https://www.paychex.com/articles/human-resources/goodbye-9-5-growth-of-the-freelance-economy

Purcell, K P J (1998) In-sourcing, outsourcing, and the growth of contingent labour as evidence of flexible employment strategies, *European Journal of Work and Organizational Psychology*, 7 (1), pp 39–59

Chapter 10

Carlson, K D and Kavanagh, M J (2012) HR metrics and workforce analytics, in *Human Resource Information Systems: Basics, Applications, and Future Directions*, eds M J Kavanagh, M Thite & R D Johnson, pp 150–174, Thousand Oaks, CA, Sage

Davenport, T H, Harris, J and Shapiro, J (2010) Competing on talent analytics, *Harvard Business Review*, 88 (10), pp 52–58

Chapter 11

Schweyer, A (2010) *Talent Management Systems: Best Practices in Technology Solutions for Recruitment, Retention and Workforce Planning*, John Wiley & Sons, Oxford

Sidhu, J (2003) Mission statements: Is it time to shelve them? *European Management Journal*, 21 (4), pp 439–46

Chapter 12

Hiatt, J (2006) *ADKAR: A Model for Change in Business, Government, and Our Community*, Prosci, Fort Collins, CO

Kotter, J P (1996) Chapters 3–10 in *Leading Change*, pp 37–153, Harvard Business Review Press, Boston

Kotter, J P (2014) Accelerate: building strategic agility for a faster-moving world in *Accelerate: Building Strategic Agility for a Faster-Moving World*, Harvard Business, Review Press, Boston

Kotter, J P and Cohen, D S (2002) *The Heart of Change: Real-Life Stories of How People Change Their Organizations*, Harvard Business Review Press, Boston

Lewin, K (2008) Quasi-stationary social equilibria and the problem of permanent change, in *Organization Change: A Comprehensive Reader*, ed W W Burke, D G Lake and J Waymire Paine, pp 73–77, Jossey-Bass, San Francisco

McKee, S (2009) *When Growth Stalls: How It Happens, Why You're Stuck, and What to Do About It*, John Wiley & Sons, Oxford

Weick, K E and Quinn, R E (1999) Organizational change and development, *Annual Review of Psychology*, 50 (1), pp 361–86

Chapter 13

Wakefield, J [accessed 17 November 2017] Foxconn Replaces '60,000 Factory Workers with Robots' [Online] http://www.bbc.com/news/technology-36376966

Phadnis, S and Ayyar, R [accessed 17 November 2017] After Cognizant, Other IT Biggies like Wipro and Infosys also Prepare for Layoffs [Online] http://economictimes.indiatimes.com/articleshow/58587158.cms

Rensi, E [accessed 17 November 2017] Thanks To 'Fight For $15' Minimum Wage, McDonald's Unveils Job-Replacing Self-Service Kiosks Nationwide [Online] https://www.forbes.com/sites/realspin/2016/11/29/thanks-to-fight-for-15-minimum-wage-mcdonalds-unveils-job-replacing-self-service-kiosks-nationwide/#4865675f4fbc

Templeton, G [accessed 17 November 2017] BlackRock Inc's Stock Trading A.I. is About to Replace Human [Online] https://www.inverse.com/article/29670-blackrock-stock-trading-program-unemployment-white-collar

Manyika, J *et al* (2017) *A Future that Works: Automation, Employment, and Productivity*, McKinsey Global Institute, New York

Long, H [accessed 17 November 2017] U.S. Has Lost 5 million Manufacturing Jobs Since 2000 [Online] http://money.cnn.com/2016/03/29/news/economy/us-manufacturing-jobs/index.html

INDEX

Note: Page numbers in *italics* refer to figures and those followed by *sum* refer to chapter summaries.
The index has followed the book's convention of using the abbreviation 'SWP' for strategic workforce plan and planning.

Printed in the USA
CPSIA information can be obtained
at www.ICGtesting.com
JSHW011905110624
64610JS00021B/710